House Beautiful

500

MAKEOVERS

Great Ideas & Quick Changes

House Beautiful

500
MAKEOVERS

Great Ideas & Quick Changes

From the Editors of *House Beautiful*

HEARST BOOKS
A division of Sterling Publishing Co., Inc.

New York / London
www.sterlingpublishing.com

Design by Areta Buk/Thumb Print

Library of Congress Cataloging-in-Publication Data is available.

10 9 8 7 6 5 4 3 2 1

Published by Hearst Books
A Division of Sterling Publishing Co., Inc.
387 Park Avenue South, New York, NY 10016

House Beautiful and Hearst Books are trademarks of Hearst Communications, Inc.

www.housebeautiful.com

For information about custom editions, special sales, premium and corporate purchases, please contact Sterling Special Sales Department at 800-805-5489 or specialsales@sterlingpublishing.com.

Distributed in Canada by Sterling Publishing
c/o Canadian Manda Group, 165 Dufferin Street
Toronto, Ontario, Canada M6K 3H6

Distributed in Australia by Capricorn Link (Australia) Pty. Ltd.
P.O. Box 704, Windsor, NSW 2756 Australia

Manufactured in China

ISBN 978-1-58816-694-4

contents

introduction

It's difficult to resist the lure of a "makeover." Everyone loves to see a room reinvented into a new and beautiful setting. But making over a room doesn't have to be about changing it completely. Nor does it require an expert dictating the terms of the redo. Instead of assuming you will need to start from scratch, think of a makeover as starting *fresh*. It's all about what you like and what you want. Approached in this way, you'll be in charge of what to tweak, change, or replace—and you can create rooms that reflect your taste and who you really are.

Even seasoned design aficionados can benefit from some expert advice every now and then. Whether you plan to work with a designer or tackle your decorating challenges on your own, the ideas on the pages that follow can fuel the process and offer inspiration along the way. Organized by basic design elements—simplicity, impact, and color, to name a few—the seven essential lessons presented in this book provide a firm foundation for any makeover project, large or small. Applied to the primary components that define a room—the surfaces, furnishings, soft touches, and accents—these lessons break down the often-daunting prospect of redoing an entire room into smaller tasks. The hundreds of accompanying photographs of beautiful spaces will also inspire you to create your dream rooms.

Whatever the scope of your project—cozy room or expansive, minor update or major overhaul—these ideas, tips, and tricks will help you clarify your vision and realize that change is easy, refreshing, and invigorating.

balance

It isn't necessary to understand the principles of classical design to appreciate the value of balance in a room. When you walk into a well-proportioned space, you'll know it—and you'll feel instinctively at ease. Symmetry (identical sconces flanking a mantel, a fixture whose size perfectly complements the table it hangs above) plays a part. But balance is also about improbable pairings: light and dark, old and new, casual and formal, masculine and feminine, large and small, hard and soft. You might not think, for example, to match a bold geometric print with a buttoned-up settee, or a radiant crystal chandelier with a rustic painted cabinet. Yet these sorts of juxtapositions keep a room from feeling one-note. Indeed, they work in concert to create a glorious harmony.

surfaces

1

Paneling that extends halfway to the ceiling— here in a two-story living room—makes a grand space feel more cozy. The beige walls above add depth and warmth.

2

A band of ornate crown molding can make a formal space even more luxurious. In this room, the floral details in the molding are picked up in the carpet and the curtains in the adjoining room. ▶

3

A tall, antique mirror— carefully arranged to be almost level with the tops of the doorframes and the crown molding—suits this room's lofty scale. ▶

4

Painted paneling and a unique railing (here made to resemble tree branches) bring texture to a stairwell. In this room, the symmetrical display of engravings and chromolithographs is equally eye-catching from a high or low vantage point. ◄

5

Establish a sense of harmony in a small space by limiting the palette to one color. The walls in this beige sitting room are covered with a pale yellow hand-painted damask wallpaper, which provides the perfect backdrop for a collection of like-colored antique furnishings.

6

Nature-inspired accents—
here stenciled leaf motifs
on a pair of built-in china
cabinets and a collection
of framed fish prints—
enliven and bring subtle
color to a white-walled
dining room. ◄

7

Rich, wooden floor-to-ceiling
china cabinets—inspired
by library shelves—are at
home in a dining room
with generous proportions.
Outfitted with sliding glass
doors and a rolling ladder,
the cupboards allow for an
impressive display.

8

Intricately patterned floor tiles painted in shades of cream, blue, and gray literally lay the groundwork for the color scheme in this sleek, modern kitchen. Varied textures—stone, metal, wood, tufted suede—enrich the cool palette.

9

Chocolate brown wood floors ground an airy kitchen and provide a lively contrast when matched with pale, gray-green cabinets and light gray honed and waxed granite countertops. ▶

10

A pale blue-and-cream checkerboard pattern painted on a wood floor becomes even more charming with age and wear. Here, a grid of overhead bleached beams reinforces the geometric design.

11

Keep a contemporary kitchen from feeling too cold by incorporating a few whimsical elements. Here, a rough-hewn wooden island painted cherry red and a bright blue oven door are juxtaposed against ebony-stained cabinets and a stainless-steel backsplash.

12

Large terra-cotta floor tiles give a breezy, Mediterranean villa–feel to a room. Here, they serve as a lovely foil for an elegant marble tub and other clean white furnishings.

13

Go the unexpected route. In this sunroom, instead of installing French doors, the owners opted for custom-designed stable doors made from Douglas fir. The wood doors also harmonize with the structure's ceiling beams and the modern furnishings. ▶

furnishings

14

Shake up styles: A mod print on a traditional English settee looks fresh; matching contemporary armchairs with plaid throw pillows have a similar effect.

15

For a serene, unfussy look in a casual space, think in pairs—here twin alabaster lamps, matching chairs upholstered in nubby pale blue fabric, dark-wood side tables—and stick to two dominant colors. ▶

16

While a pair of vintage stools covered in chocolate-colored leather might blend into one setting, they gain presence amidst luminous white silk upholstery. The brown hue is picked up on tables scattered throughout the room.

17

Set up separate seating areas to help break up a large living room. Here, a graceful sofa and a pair of chairs flank the fireplace, while a fabric-draped table surrounded by upholstered benches provides a spot for books and magazines.

18

Hints of bright red pop against a backdrop of neutral furnishings in solids and patterns. Consider using the hue on throw pillows and seat cushions, and in surprising ways, such as peaking out from behind a set of curtains.

19

When a living room is dominated by one feature—here, a large, open fireplace—choose furniture that balances the scale of that feature, such as this oversized sofa.

20

This great room may be done in all neutrals, but it's anything but plain. Consider upholstering matching sofas in several, subtly different fabrics. Here, the sofas feature gold fabric for the body, a pear shade for the seat cushions, and olive for the back cushions. ▶

21

For a dramatic effect, look for a chandelier with a diameter that is approximately equal to that of the table it hangs above. The sinuous shape and rough, bleached finish on this fixture—found at a flea market—give it an elegant yet natural feel. ▶

22

It's never dull to combine pieces made of the same materials—here warm, ruddy wood—so long as each item has a distinct personality. In this foyer, an antique carved mirror, ornate console table, and English wheelback chairs all hold their own.

23

Expand the dimensions of
a space by incorporating
mirrors in unexpected ways.
In this entry, an embellished
antique oval piece is placed
above a marble-topped
console table with a square
mirror mounted underneath.

24

It may seem counter-intuitive to pair modern linen-upholstered chairs with a heavy antique mahogany dining table, but here it works beautifully. Note how the gray of the chairs is picked up in the mural and the rich tone of the wood is repeated on the sideboard. ◄ ◄

25

A stately antique elm trestle table and warm leather-upholstered chairs anchor this sunny kitchen. ◄

26

Sumptuous tufted suede chairs and a crystal chandelier look luxurious when set against a spare fireplace, simple antique hutch, and tile floors in a breakfast nook.

27

Masculine (glossy black
shelves, bull-fighting
imagery) meets feminine
(floral-print wrap-around
sofa) in this cozy den.
The lattice style of the
shelves keeps them from
seeming heavy. ◄

28

Create a glamorous,
ethereal look in a guest
bedroom to promote
comfort and relaxation—
achieved here with a
champagne-colored chaise,
glass baluster tables that
practically disappear, and
diaphanous curtains.

soft touches

29

Using one dominant color and pattern enables you to mix styles with ease. Here, traditional plaid upholstery mingles effortlessly with a mod concentric square rug. The geometric theme is echoed in the light fixture and the boxy silhouettes of the dining chairs. ◄

30

For a contemporary look, consider hanging the curtains for two windows (situated along the same wall) from a single rod. Generous fabric panels mounted several inches above the window frames create a sense of drama.

31

Make a cozy room feel more spacious by mounting large-scale wall hangings just below ceiling height. Here, a pair of coordinating Asian silk hangings—flanking a bleached oak entertainment unit—draws the eye upward.

32

When combining multiple patterns, think in terms of scale. In this colorful living room, a splashy floral print on the upholstery, medium-size lattice pattern on the carpet, and tiny checks on the curtains and pillows work in harmony. ▶

33

Another way to connect otherwise incongruous patterns is with trim. Here, red piping and grosgrain ribbon accent the cushions and skirts (respectively) on the upholstered pieces, while thick scarlet fringe surrounds the pillows. ▶

34

Unify a diverse collection of furnishings—here an elegant English recamier and four styles of chairs—with a single upholstery pattern. Ties connecting fabric and cushions to frames lend a pretty, feminine touch. ◄

35

Regal gold curtains provide a warm counterpoint to bare floors and a cool pattern. Two rows of braid finished with fringe on the box-pleated valances echo the small embellishments on the slipcovers. ◄

36

Upholstered dining chairs make an ornate breakfast nook feel cozy. In this room, the soft, sandy hues of the fabric, floor, and zinc chandelier, sparked in places by bits of gold, create a serene environment.

37

Give a motif an almost three-dimensional effect by layering matching patterns, as seen here on the walls, upholstered headboard, bed skirt, and curtain swag in a child's room. The bed seems less obtrusive when blended in with its surroundings—ideal in a tight space.

38

Patterned fabrics are typically used for bedclothes, but try them on a headboard and dust ruffle for a cozy look. Matching curtains help tie this room together, while a quilted coverlet and solid-colored chair and ottoman add texture. ▶

39

Frame a bed or other beautiful piece of furniture by arranging it between two windows, each dressed with a single curtain panel (instead of the familiar pair) swept to one side. ◂◂

40

If there's a pattern you absolutely love, go all out with it. Here, a toile Roman shade and duvet cover—defined with a wide black trim—extend the wallpaper pattern in a cozy guest bedroom. Buffalo check fabric on the chairs provides graphic contrast. ◂

41

Curtains aren't just for windows. Suspended from a track mounted around the perimeter of the ceiling, they can also envelop a room with texture and softness.

42

Ensure a monochromatic room is never monotonous by choosing pieces in a range of materials—in this case stone, wood, and mirror, along with plush shag carpeting.

accents

43

Avoid hanging pictures too high, which can look awkward and force viewers to crane their necks. The center of this antique Italian fresco is at eye level and doesn't quite clear the pillows on the bench below—a casual touch in a formal entryway.

44

Let a room's dominant design elements, such as architecture or wallpaper, dictate how you decorate. In this foyer, ladder-like étagères mimic the pattern of the windows around the front door.

45

A colorful, crisply pleated tablecloth in a dramatic floral print brightens a table in a foyer. Topped with a sheet of 1/4-inch-thick glass, cut to fit, the fabric topper serves as a lovely base for seasonal floral displays.

46

In a pale, neutral room, a handful of dark pieces— such as flea-market prints in black-and-gold frames and bamboo chairs painted a shiny ebony hue—provide focal points. ◄

47

Complement symmetrical aspects of a room—here, a door located in the center of a wall—by mirroring arrangements. In this room, two pairs of antique lithographs and two iron console tables both topped with gleaming gold lamps, are identically arranged on each side of the door.

48

A pair of ornately patterned lighting fixtures brings a touch of old-world glamour to a room dominated by clean lines and modern shapes. In this room, the abstract pattern on the rug echoes the design of the cables used to suspend the lamps.

49

Let a magnificent view—here of a sweeping lawn and the ocean in the distance—take center stage by installing window treatments that won't compete for attention; neutral colors work best. ▶

50

Create an intriguing mantel display by mixing elaborate pieces—intricately carved pagodas, a lavish gold frame—with more humble ones. These simple, basket-weave bud vases are filled with cheerful red ranunculus.

51

Towering arrangements of flowering branches (which here reiterate the motif on the wall), window treatments that hang to the floor, and a set of mirrors help make a small space appear roomier. ▶

52

Not all artwork has to be hung. A series of prints propped up on a mantel feels modern and refreshingly informal. Bright hydrangeas set in the fireplace below offset the black-and-white scheme.

53

Ornate antique candlesticks bring a Baroque twist to a simple dining table. Arranging a few collectibles at one end of the table, instead of a pair in the center, looks less expected and won't block diners' views.

54

Small pictures have greater impact when displayed en masse. These eighteenth-century watercolors are arranged in tight rows—just like the beams overhead. The works fill a whole wall, to stunning effect. ▶

55

This large, eat-in nook has two shades on each window—the lower can be closed for privacy while the upper remains open, allowing some natural light into the room. Or they can both be closed for complete privacy.

56

Mix and match different styles and eras for an eclectic table setting. Here, a new patterned teacup mingles gracefully with a vintage salad plate, Danish stoneware dinner plate, and chopstick-like utensils that were found at a flea market.

57

A few colorful dishes
invigorate a collection of
white china and make for
an eye-catching, whimsical
display when arranged
inside window cabinets
or on open shelving. ◄

58

Bring outdoor-style
lighting indoors. Here,
unfussy metal Colonial
lanterns look right at home
in a classic, wood-paneled
kitchen. Twice the size
of traditional lanterns, the
fixtures complement the
spacious interior.

59

Bathroom walls inlaid with mirrors create a dazzling effect when the lights are on. In this room, the white-painted cabinetry, gleaming floor, and shiny metal of the lamps enhance the brightness.

60

A mostly white color scheme, metal side table, and sleek cabinet hardware lend a modern edge to a bathroom with rustic architecture. ▶

61

Consider how the aspects of a bathroom work together. Here, a freestanding vessel sink harmonizes with the luxurious soaking tub. ▶

62

Natural materials and accents look, well, natural on a sunporch. Stone, wicker, distressed wood, and plants atop antique pedestals define this sunny space.

outdoors

63

Create a dramatic entry into a pool—here, a lush archway—by framing the steps with potted greenery such as small palm trees in giant urns. In this scenario, large planters also anchor the pool's opposite corners.

64

Break up a sweeping, sloped landscape—and make it easier to navigate—with sets of stone steps. These can be as artful as this semicircular design or as simple as the linear ledges beyond.

65

A formal garden is more engaging when you mix materials (weathered wood, stone) and shapes (rectangular, oval, and circular hedges, triangular obelisks). Here, the steps leading to a trellis-backed platform are reminiscent of an open-air theater. ▶

66

A textural border of mixed grasses, shrubs, and plants with variegated leaves helps define a broad lawn. Choose flowers that bloom at different times throughout the year.

67

A pool blends in with the landscape when surrounded by a simple wood deck and tall meadow plants such as goldenrod and orchard grasses. ▶

CHAPTER 2

simplicity

Take a hard look at the rooms in your home. Do the majority of pieces in them bring you joy? If not, it's time to consider how you might pare down or rearrange the space. This isn't about turning every interior into a sterile, minimalist shrine; instead, think of it as creating an environment where the things you love can shine. It can be very freeing, for example, to remove the curtains from a window, taking full advantage of a spectacular view, or to pull up a busy area rug and discover how much more beautiful the carved legs of a sofa look against the bare floor. Also give some thought to the weight of your pieces. Floating shelves, a china cabinet filled with clear glassware, and Lucite chairs are all functional without feeling heavy or overwhelming. By designing a space where your items have room to breathe, you too will breathe easier.

surfaces

68

Put the spotlight on an elegant staircase by choosing a creamy paint, a pale lime-stone floor, and a judicious mix of furnishings (note the almost completely bare walls and unadorned window in this entryway). ◄

69

Give walls texture and depth—and eliminate the need for a lot of artwork—by covering them with Venetian plaster, a substance that is applied with a trowel and then burnished for a stucco-like effect.

70

One of the simplest ways to warm a modern interior (other than with a roaring fire) is with a soft, fluffy rug.

71

A few organic elements, such as the branch and plants used here, can also breathe life into a living room with a monochromatic palette—here, off-white.

72

Accents with reflective surfaces—a floor-to-ceiling mirror and crystal chandelier and table lamps—infuse a room with glamour. In this living area, serene, gray-blue furnishings ensure the look doesn't become too glitzy. ▶

73
Here, limestone floors, white walls, and shaded floor-to-ceiling windows keep the atmosphere cool in the media room of a South Beach condominium.

74

Stock open shelves with clear glassware to keep a small pantry from feeling cluttered. Whitewashed cabinetry and a pale marble countertop contribute to the clean, airy vibe.

75

Imbue a mostly white kitchen with bright splashes of color—such as the green glass cabinet doors here. The geometric pattern of the Carrara marble–topped island is repeated on the slate floors and large window beyond.

76

Kitchen cupboards become like pieces of furniture when embellished with cornices and raised paneling. Here, the asymmetrical design of the panels—echoed in the stone floor tiles—lends a modern touch in keeping with the sleek stainless-steel appliances. ▶

77

Cool soapstone counter-
tops and a honey-colored
island help lighten a room
dominated by rich, dark-wood
cabinetry. Delicate hardware
keeps the cupboards from
feeling bulky. ◄

78

Small, pretty details—
curved brackets, delicate
muntins, gathered
curtains—give kitchen
cabinets feminine charm . . .

79

. . . that is kept in check
by olive green paint and
a glossy black soapstone
backsplash and countertops.

80

Floating shelves, which
take up less space than
wall-mounted cabinets, are
ideal in a narrow kitchen.
Display only what you
use regularly, along with
a few decorative items, and
relegate everything else to
a cupboard or drawer. ◄

81

Custom built-in millwork—
here floor-to-ceiling shelves,
sliding doors, lots of drawers,
and a built-in desk with
a walnut veneer—can
transform a hallway into
a sleek home office.

82

Cleaner than curtains and more decorative than shades, Shoji screens—here made of the same amber-colored wood as the door frames—soften the sunlight and set a zen tone.

83

Consider painting not just walls, but ceilings too, to magnify the color's impact. Here, the soothing qualities of lilac-gray make a room look more finished.

84

Nearly every surface in this dazzling, romantic bathroom shines: The walls are made of white milk glass, the cabinet doors feature mirrored panes, and the floor is lined with glass mosaic tiles. Even the woodwork gleams, thanks to high-gloss paint.

85

Cover not only a shower stall but also the wall beyond with aqua glass mosaic tiles to give a bathroom an ethereal, watery look. Here, the tiles also connect the transparent shower with the white soaking tub, making them feel less disjointed. ▶

furnishings

86

You can enliven any room simply by arranging the furniture in unexpected ways. This asymmetrical walnut-aluminum-and-Plexiglas coffee table looks surprising in a space with rustic architecture; positioning the table so that it's perpendicular to the sofas and overhead beams gives it extra edge. ◄

87

Make any living space— be it an entry, hallway, or family room—feel cozier by setting up a reading area. You don't need much: just a comfy chair, a warm throw, and a few books arranged on shelves or a table.

88

In a room with a stunning view, choose low, streamlined furnishings and let the view take center stage. Here, a glass cube coffee table—its shape echoed by boxy rope chairs—beautifully mirrors a sweeping window.

89

A graceful all-white entryway
is an ideal canvas for a dark
table with gorgeous lines, like
this antique wood-topped
metal piece. Its slanted
legs and V-shaped support
contrast nicely with the
elegant turned balusters
and vertical paneling.

90

If you really want to embrace simplicity, leave the white walls in a large room almost completely bare. ◄

91

A collection of keenly edited furnishings can update a traditional room. Here, a refined settee is freshened with a subtle stripe and paired with armchairs covered in creamy solid fabrics. Set atop a sisal rug, they look elegant but not overly formal.

92

Create a light, airy
scene with furnishings
that seem to float: a coffee
table with a clear base that
disappears, a sofa with legs
hidden behind a side table,
a wall-mounted TV. Chairs
with lots of space beneath
them contribute to the
breezy look.

93

Rustic teak benches are a
great choice for a covered
porch: They mix nicely with
other wood finishes and
upholstered pieces, and can
be used for outdoor seating
when needed. ▶

94

Here's a fresh take on upholstery—covering not just seat cushions and backs, but legs (or arms) too. Whereas dark-wood chair legs would look chaotic beneath a table like this one, wrapping them in lime green fabric lets the elegant, five-prong stand shine.

95

A dining room need not be formal. Simple director's chairs—more commonly seen on patios or in game rooms—are an ideal match for a table with X-supports. The grid pattern on the canvas echoes the grilles on the windows, which are intentionally left bare to make the most of the view. ▶

96

An armless sofa has the feeling of a banquette when pulled up to a breakfast room table. A trio of Lucite chairs is a pleasing counterpoint to the solid upholstery.

97

Design a dual-purpose space for dining and relaxing by pairing an unfussy, lightweight table (such as this bamboo one) and chairs with a long sofa. When it's not needed, the table can easily be moved aside.

98

Turn a beautiful table,
like this antique one,
into a charming bathroom
countertop: have an
opening cut for a drainpipe,
purchase a vessel sink and
faucets, and let a plumber
do the rest.

soft touches

99

Mix soft, richly tactile materials—a corrugated silk-wool rug, ultra-suede, and faille upholstery—to create a sumptuous, enticing effect.

100

The idea of crisp white upholstery is alluring, but in reality it's not always practical. Washable canvas slipcovers, used here on the sofa, chairs, and ottomans, are a low-maintenance solution. ◄

101

Small details—such as the pretty, feminine pleats and gathered scalloped edges on this pair of Roman shades— become more important and noticeable in a spare space.

102

In a modern scheme, consider not only avant-garde styles but also innovative materials as well. This richly colored rug looks like shag, but it's actually made from felt.

103

By layering solid curtain panels over gauzy sheers, which tend to have a more delicate look than shades, you can give windows dimension and control the amount of light in a room. ▶

104

A custom-made mantel-
piece can add substance
to the living room of
a Mediterranean-style
home. ◄

105

A buttery rug made of
heavy wool sets a luxurious
tone. Here, full, billowy
curtains, ornate furnishings,
and fringed pillows follow
suit. ◄

106

In a room with dramatic
architecture, curtains with
a tasseled fringe provide a
hint of embellishment
without being over-the-top.
Here, the rich hue of the
fringe echoes the color of
the arched beams above.

107

When designing a room, many interior decorators say they choose the carpet first because it makes subsequent decisions easier. Here, a colorful, graphic rug is the showpiece; the other furnishings are kept simple so as not to compete with it.

108

Subtle textures from sheer
waffle-weave curtain panels,
a linen-upholstered chair,
and the brushstrokes on an
abstract painting warm a
creamy, minimalist space.

109

Infuse texture into an elegantly spare dining room with window treatments that feature subtle details. In this room, plain curtain panels are topped with pencil-pleats and their leading edges are trimmed with a long, luxurious trim.

110

Create a cohesive look by dressing all of the windows in a room—even French doors—with the same curtains. Mounting panels above the frame makes grandiose architecture, such as the doors shown here, appear even more magnificent. ▶

111

Unlike slipcovers or upholstery, curtains and throw pillows offer a relatively low-commitment way to incorporate pattern in a bedroom or any space. When you tire of them or the seasons change, simply trade them for something new.

112

Consider accenting a graceful four-poster with fabric-draped walls instead of a canopy. Generous pleats give the room texture without obscuring the bed's elegant shape. ▶

113

Luxury doesn't have to be showy. A plush tufted bed frame and subtly patterned rug and chair, all in quiet shades of gray-blue and ivory, transform a bedroom into a dreamy, deluxe retreat. ◄

114

Roman shades that can be drawn from the bottom up— permitting privacy without blocking light—are ideal in a ground-floor space. Narrow valances balance the look.

accents

115

Pile birch logs vertically inside a fireplace (this one is constructed from smooth limestone) for a look that's both decorative and practical. Just rearrange the logs and remove any extras when you're ready to light a flame.

116

It's sometimes helpful to think of a room in terms of light and shadows. Here, bright white upholstery offsets a dark arrangement composed of primitive pottery, giant shells, and a heavy wooden table and carved mirror. ▶

117

Some of the most intriguing displays don't cost a penny. Pinecones, birch logs, and twigs found in the yard and heaped into a wooden vessel soften a contemporary space.

118

Upholstered in Castel's Zoe, a lustrous fabric in a lively chartreuse hue, the sculptural lines of this beautiful nineteenth-century English settee stand out. Bolsters covered in the same fabric add another elegant touch.

119

Take care not to overdo a theme. In this living room, a pair of fanciful carved wooden seahorses and a bowlful of shells—set atop a pale cypress cabinet—are all that's needed to create a breezy, beachy vibe.

120

An ornate fireplace needs
little adornment. In this
room, a simple Art Deco
mirror—whose protruding
shape complements that
of the mantel—unfussy
sconces, and a smattering
of accessories are just
right. ◀

121

An appealing vignette
depends not just on the
beautiful items you choose,
but also on how you arrange
them. In this scenario, a pair
of square pillows echoes the
shape of the gilded mirror,
while the rectangular pillow
mimics the lines of the
antique striped bench.

122

Keep small vases on a mantel or table and continually rotate in blooms and branches—such as this trio of leaning orchid branches—from the garden or market.

123

Here's one way to chart a new decorating course. Divide an oversize map— here an antique map of Paris—into equal sections. Frame each piece and reassemble them on a wall for a stunning display. ▶

124

Architectural salvage companies are great places to look for interesting flourishes that can be used in lieu of artwork—such as this eighteenth-century Corinthian column.

125

Use bold shapes sparingly. In this kitchen, the carved wood posts, curved doorway, and range hood create a distinct and beautiful look. ▶

126

Just because a kitchen is a workspace doesn't mean it has to be void of artistic touches. These pendant lamps are a perfect blend of form and function, providing elegant modern shapes and focused light over a countertop. ◄◄

127

Narrow mirrors mounted over separate washbasins make a small bathroom ideal for two. The glass reflects light from the adjacent shaded sconces.

outdoors

128

The glassy surface of an infinity pool set against a woodsy backdrop doubles the beauty of the surroundings.

129

Al fresco spaces, such as this rooftop terrace done up in bright pink hues, are good spots to experiment with daring colors. ▶

130

An all-weather carpet cuts down on glare from floor tiles and lays the foundation for a welcoming outdoor room. ▶

131

A streamlined pool house clad in cedar boards doesn't intrude on a leafy landscape. The structure's beauty—the varying colors of the wood, the way a louvered canopy casts slanted shadows on the facade—is natural and understated.

132

Convert a deck outside the master bedroom of a weekend house into an outdoor shower. Here, the deck is framed by a tall cast-concrete wall on one side and an unfinished cedar wall equipped with the showerhead on the other. ▶

133

Weathered teak benches
and dining chairs appear
almost camouflaged when
arranged on gray stone
ledges, offering a natural
backdrop for a pool.
Here, the irregular stones
complement the pool's
amorphous shape.

134

Get creative in your garden.
Flowers needn't be grown
in a bed or planter—here,
Verbena bonariensis spring
through an opening in the
center of a millstone. ▶

135

In a sprawling yard, keep
things simple by planting
low-maintenance flowers
that don't need much
tending to. ▶▶

CHAPTER 3

impact

You can have a room filled with beautiful things, but if it doesn't have that unexpected touch, that wow factor, it might still fail to make an impression. Remember the old Duke Ellington song, "It Don't Mean a Thing (If It Ain't Got that Swing)"? You might think of your space that way and aim to infuse it with a bold, rhythmic pattern, on the walls, ceiling, or floor. Or go for a singular, more nuanced gesture: a vibrant, contemporary painting in a traditionally furnished room or a gorgeous, salvage door hung on the wall like art. Some dramatic ideas—such as painting the panels on a formal fireplace a bright or contrasting hue—cost next to nothing to create, and yet, as Ellington put it, they provide that "something else that makes the tune complete."

surfaces

136

In a traditional room with mahogany paneling, one expects a solid, creamy ceiling, perhaps dressed up with an elaborate fixture—which is exactly why the playfully patterned ceiling in this room is so striking.

137

Create the feeling of two distinct spaces by painting the walls above and below a staircase in different colors. ▶

138

Make a bold statement by pitting two contrasting patterns against each other. One way to do it successfully is to assign a color palette to each print— here red and beige for the stripes and black and white for the checkerboard— then mix and match as you please. ◄

139

A floor painted with concentric squares in sandy hues provides a neutral yet energetic canvas for colorful furnishings. The soft shapes of the splashy blooms and button-tufting are a nice counterpoint to the geometric design.

140

From wooden ceiling coffers lined with woven cane to ribbed leather ottomans, nearly every surface in this Moroccan-inspired media room is infused with pattern and texture. It works because the motifs conform to a defined color palette and are all relatively small in scale.

141

Bet you never thought of burlap as elegant. But that's just the way it appears when hand-stenciled and applied to the walls of this living room. The cloth's rich texture and honey shade warm the lofty space. ▶

142

Update a traditional fireplace with contrasting paint and tiles. Here, decorative panels have been painted in glossy black. The shape and shades of the tiles inspired the colors for the wall and ceiling.

143

Venetian plaster, popularly used in the palaces of fifteenth-century Venice, conveys a sense of majesty when combined with formal furnishings and gilt accessories. Here, the finish is paired with matching wainscoting for added interest. ▶

144

An outdoor motif—such as the lattice-print on the sideboard and hand-painted walls of this cheerful dining room—looks fresh in a formal space. The plaid chair backs and subtle squares on the floor echo the geometric design.

Reinvigorate a classic wallpaper print, such as this toile, by installing it above wainscoting. Bright accents, like the lime green paint used on the back of a bookshelf, heighten the effect.

146

Coordinate patterns on walls and floors for a polished, multidimensional feel—here, the oversize circular print on the wall-covering complements the small hexagonal floor tiles in this Mediterranean-inspired space. ◄

147

Bright paint on the floor can put an original twist on a traditional pattern—such as the folk art hex sign shown here—and keeps a country-style room from feeling quaint.

148

A striking collection deserves a proper perch. Here, colorful antique porcelain hens roost on a shelf rimming a break-fast nook, as well as in niches between windows. A wirework basket that was converted into a chandelier reinforces the country theme.

149
A tiled checkerboard
backsplash brings retro
punch to a kitchen.
A recessed shelf treated
with the same pattern is
practically indiscernible
and has the effect of an
optical illusion.

150
With a little imagination, a piece designed for one purpose can be tasked with another. This gorgeous marble counter, found at a salvage shop, was once used for storing and serving ice cream at a diner.

151

A traditional print, such as this pineapple one, becomes modern when used in a large scale. Understated, organic colors and materials allow the motif to take center stage. ◄

152

Give a den the feeling of a contemporary hunting lodge with faux-bois wallpaper and an artful display of antlers. (These were purchased at an online auction.) Dark wood and other natural materials enhance the look.

153

Create the dreamy look of an enchanted forest in a bedroom with a lush vine motif on the walls. This design is hand-painted, but wallpaper would work equally well. Slanted surfaces give the print a three-dimensional appearance.

154

Wallpaper with a bold, busy print, such as this toile, softens the edges of an irregularly shaped room. Papering a recessed nook offers a cozy spot for a desk. ▶

155

Evoke the sense of having a canopy of blossoms overhead by papering the walls and sloped ceiling in a bedroom with a pretty floral print. Vases of fresh blooms and flowering branches enhance the effect.

156

Rich textures (such as this grasscloth ceiling) and patterns (leopard-print, plaids, stripes, florals) spice up a strict three-color palette. ▶

157

Wallpaper rendered in soft shades and with lots of space between motifs—such as this hand-painted garden scene—has a relaxing effect that's ideal for a bedroom. ◄

158

Rows of mirrored panels make a sophisticated alternative to a headboard. These mirrors are silvered, which lends an aged, smoky patina.

159

A swirling mosaic pattern on the floor makes a whitewashed bathroom come alive. The curved lines of the light fixture reiterate the motif, while the large photograph fleshes out the nature theme. ◄◄

160

Make the most of natural light in a bathroom by covering surfaces with a highly reflective material, such as the gleaming caramel-colored onyx seen here on the floors, tub deck, and walls of the double shower. ◄

161

When stripes are a dominant theme, as these contrasting limestone and marble ones are, opt for patterns that alternate narrow and wide bands. These tend to be more visually appealing than broad patterns of equal proportions.

162

Lessen the formality of a stately piece and the room it occupies with a casual display. On this antique secretary, old books, framed photos, and silver curios are arranged haphazardly on purpose.

163

A chaise longue is the ultimate comfy seat, but putting more than one in a room isn't always practical. Here, a quartet of more compact chairs with reclining backs and long seats lets several people relax at once. ▶

164

The most intriguing furnishings often come from humble beginnings. This dramatically curved tufted settee was bought for a song at a thrift store and reupholstered in eye-catching floral ticking. ◄

165

Be flexible when mounting pictures above a piece of furniture. Whereas a traditional row or square of frames would seem odd paired with this heart-shape settee, a grouping that echoes its form looks just right. ◄

166

A leafy chintz, with all of its intricate details—shadows, subtle color variations, tiny veins and stems—lights up when set against dark walls.

167

Give a beautiful dining set the attention it deserves by contrasting it with its surroundings. This elegant whitewashed table and chairs shine in a room with scarlet walls and heavy, patterned curtains. ◄

168

Transform a workaday picnic table into a chic indoor dining table. Here, one is painted a shiny lime green. Its benches are topped with chocolate brown cushions and pleated skirts trimmed with matching green braid.

169

Everyone gathers in the kitchen, so install a table that doubles as a work surface and a casual place to dine. This fourteen-foot-long marble-topped piece with stools arranged on two sides serves both purposes beautifully.

170

A patterned table made from a synthetic material, such as this pretty laminate one, is a smart touch in a kitchen. You'll never need a tablecloth, and the surface is a breeze to clean and care for. ▶

171

Red can energize just about
any space. To keep it from
feeling racy in a traditional
room, combine it with
classic patterns and materials
like the plaids and crewel
fabric in this library. ◀

172

Cool blue unites a range
of patterns—boldly striped
armchairs, polka-dot curtains,
delicately embellished tiles
and china—in this seductive
bedroom nook.

173

This headboard scales new heights. Made of mahogany and embellished with a nickel grid that ties in with the metal on the spiky lamps, it stretches from floor to ceiling, bringing drama to a bedroom. ◀

174

Here are two novel ideas: a wrap-around upholstered headboard that neatly embraces a bed as well as its side tables; and a footboard-cum-settee that masterfully blends form and function.

soft touches

175

Curtains with linings have a dramatic, full look, provide insulation, and resist fading better than unlined styles. Viewed from the outside, a lining also tends to be more visually appealing than the reverse side of a pattern.

176

Consider this fresh way to play with pattern: Place a small, narrow-stripe rug, slightly askew, over a larger carpet with bigger stripes. Add colorful upholstery and throw pillows in a variety of motifs (plaid, leopard print) for a vibrant, eclectic look. ▶

177

Instead of a coffee table, try using a pair of giant floor pillows (these feature an eye-catching embroidered design) to anchor a seating area. The cushions can hold board games or drinks on a tray and serve as extra seating when needed.

178

Make a small window feel larger by hanging curtains several inches away from the frame on either side, as seen on the right in this photo. ▶

179

Showcase beautiful quilts— and bring extra layers of color and warmth to upholstered furnishings—by draping the coverlets over a sofa or large ottoman. ▶

180

Just because you've chosen an elaborately patterned rug doesn't mean the furnishings you pair with it have to be solid or neutral. Stripes and florals, drawn from the carpet's palette, can also work harmoniously. ◀

181

Vibrant colors and patterns add drama to a double-height living room. Here, boldly patterned fabrics pep up a wing chair and a French neoclassical daybed. Velvet curtains and a red area rug add energy to the mix of antique furnishings.

182

Complement a lavishly intricate rug, such as this Persian one, with other opulent pieces: billowy curtains, tufted cushions, a crystal chandelier, an elaborately painted mirror.

183

Canvas trim gives these bright, richly textured chenille Roman shades a crisp, modern edge. The shape goes well with clean, utilitarian-style windows. ▶

184

A band of cornflower-blue silk at the base of a luminous pale blue silk shade adds weight and keeps the light fabric from getting lost beneath abundant patterned curtains.

185

The most luxurious window treatments and bed canopies have hems that pool slightly on the floor. For an extravagant drape, choose curtains with a combined width of about three times that of the window.

186

Give bed canopies a
charming, layered look
with contrasting fabrics.
A column of embroidered
cloth lined with a cheerful
check—which matches the
headboard and footboard—
crowns a twin bed in this
cozy guest room.

187

Less expected than wallpaper or paint, fabric-covered walls lend texture and warmth to a room. Choose a pretty, printed design, like this Indian one, and you won't need many other decorations or artwork. ◄

188

Here's an alternative to artwork in a frame: mounting a gorgeous fabric behind a canopy bed. Here, a shimmery, mirrored canopy and quilted silk coverlet provide dazzling counterpoints to the matte cloth.

189

A waterfall of box-pleated silk creates a glamorous backdrop for a bed. The one in this room is hung from a cornice cleverly aligned with the ceiling molding.

190

Sometimes a room designed around simple themes—primary colors, geometric shapes—has the greatest visual impact. Here, the angular lines of the bed and box-pleated valances stand in stark contrast to the rounded forms of the tables, as well as the lamps and circles on the rug. ▶

191

Make store-bought items your own. In this young boy's room, a custom padded Ultrasuede headboard softens a streamlined steel bed. ▶

192

Bring near-Eastern flair to a bedroom with a large-scale paisley pattern, a motif that originated in Persia. Delicate fringe adds softness to the curtains and canopy, which also features a fleecy chenille liner.

193

Give any bed the stature and softness of a canopied four-poster by installing gathered panels topped with a valance around the headboard. A luxurious velvet lining provides the curtains with weight and fullness. ▶

accents

194

Give a beautiful lamp greater presence with a well-placed mirror. The elegant mirror in this photo reflects a striking iron-and-glass chandelier from the nineteenth century. Truncated columns topped with hydrangea-filled tin urns contribute to the grand look.

195

A classically furnished room doesn't require a Wyeth or Renoir. Contemporary art, especially a colorful piece juxtaposed against neutral surroundings, also shines. ▶

196

Add a temporary new color—here green—to a room's palette by coordinating matching flowers and even fresh fruit. ▶

197

Never mind that your home didn't come with decorative molded panels and other distinctive details. Create your own grand architectural elements by hanging a beautiful salvage piece, like this eighteenth-century carved Italian door.

198

Distinguished architecture calls for accessories of the same caliber, such as a textural relief wall sculpture instead of framed pictures, or a folding screen covered in rich leather rather than more conventional fabric. ▶

199

Draw attention to collectibles
by displaying them in a glass
case. This one, with a vibrant
slatted-wood background,
harmonizes with the vertical
lines of the paneling on the
walls, ceiling, and floor, and
the striped rug. ◄

200

Use accessories to dress up
and define an unadorned
fireplace. Here, an ornate
antique carved-wood mirror
is placed at about mantel-
height, while a pair of floor
lamps delineates a hearth.

201

A grouping of like artifacts from different cultures—here ornate Mexican crosses and a selection of Italian ex-votos—makes for a dynamic tabletop display.

202

Instead of covering all of the walls in a room with hand-painted wallpaper, which can be pricy, consider framing pieces from a single roll or remnant and using them as art. Gorgeous fabric panels also work well.

203

Handsome ceiling fixtures, which draw the eye up, can be used to highlight interesting architecture such as moldings, a pretty tin pattern, or in this case, a network of exposed beams. ◄

204

A photograph makes a bold statement when enlarged to mural-size. This one was cut into pieces and reassembled, creating a grid with graphic, modern appeal.

205

Artwork with a soft, repeating motif (Cy Twombly's *Roman Notes*, shown here, resembles a handwritten missive) is a lovely foil for geometric-pattern upholstery.

206

A selection of whale vertebrae might be among the last things you'd expect to see arranged beneath an elegant glass chandelier, but the glamorous-meets-gritty look is surprisingly appealing.

207

Chinoiserie pieces have a sophistication that allows them to blend effortlessly with traditional decor. Here, an intricate copper lantern and a collection of ginger jars and other Asian-inspired objects infuse a dining room with romance.

208

A luminous clear-glass chandelier appears even more ethereal floating above a landscape of dark-wood furnishings. A pale oak table balances the look. ▶

209

You can build a whole room around one gorgeous piece. A brilliant antique Guatemalan water container, used to hold blankets, influenced the color of the walls, duvet cover, and artwork in this blissful guest bedroom.

210

Need an easy, inexpensive way to display art en masse? Cut pictures, such as these illustrated nature studies, from a book and arrange them in frames. A black-and-white photo of leopard cubs harmonizes with the fanciful yet refined scheme in a young boy's room. ▶

211

When it comes to sheer glamour, nothing beats Art Deco–style mirrored pieces. Match them with antiques, such as the bergère here, for a luxurious look in a bathroom or bedroom. ◂◂

212

Hang a large decorative mirror to brighten a dark bathroom. It will reflect natural light during the day and, in this room, the dazzling glow from a crystal chandelier at night. ◂

213

A giant, decorative mirror—of the sort more commonly seen in a living or dining area—looks fresh in a bathroom. Its reflective surface also helps expand the dimensions of a small space.

214

Your home is supposed to bring you joy, so go ahead and indulge your whims. In this pool house, a quirky "Funny Boy" sign and pen-and-ink drawing of the actor Nathan Lane pay homage to *The Producers*.

215

An old barn can be transformed into a stunning space for an indoor pool. This structure, which boasts its original Pennsylvania bluestone walls, is furnished with comfy wicker pieces. ▶

outdoors

216

You can make a big splash in a small backyard: consider this modern checkerboard patio framed by a rose-edged lily pond.

217

For an exalted look, try installing an arcade, like this teak one, and covering it with a variety of light-filtering, climbing blooms such as wisteria, clematis, and roses.

218

Like rooms, gardens don't have to conform to one style. A mix of shrubs, ferns, grasses, water-loving fronds, even a tall 'Green Arrow' Weeping Alaskan cedar, infuse this scene with personality. ▶

CHAPTER 4

function

If you've ever looked at the expertly designed rooms in a decorating book or magazine and thought "yeah right, that would never work in *my* home," this chapter is for you. While it's wonderful to have a gorgeous space with dramatic flair, you still have to live there. Luckily, there are plenty of tricks you can employ to make a room both beautiful and practical. Have a busy (or boisterous) family? Learn about scratch-resistant stone, durable upholstery fabric, and smart storage solutions. Short on space? Set up a home office or library in an existing room or underutilized nook. Need a place to zone out at the end of the day? Create the serene, sumptuous bedroom you've always dreamed of. Now *that's* what life is all about.

surfaces

219

Wall paneling, which is readily available at home supply stores, is an easy way to bring character to a room lacking architectural details. ◄

220

Cover a playroom wall with chalkboard paint to ensure the surface is ready whenever inspiration strikes young artists. Other smart touches include pint-size furniture and a beige cotton carpet that camouflages minor stains.

221

Rich, espresso-brown walls, set off by bright white doors and trim, envelop a casual dining area in warmth. In this room, textured bamboo shades and a sisal rug bridge the contrasting hues. ◄

222

When it comes to creating an elegant look, less is often more. Graceful, dark-wood furnishings, simple striped seats, and a coat of khaki-colored paint on the walls make this room beautiful and livable.

223

Keep wood floors gleaming with occasional damp mopping. (Never saturate the surface with water.) Most wood floors are finished with polyurethane, a protective coating, and don't need to be waxed. Unfinished floors, or those treated with varnish or shellac, should be waxed once or twice a year.

224

Think of solid surfacing materials, such as the pale green Corian on this island, as the ultimate in luxurious yet low-maintenance countertop options. These man-made surfaces look like stone but require no polishing, sealing, or special cleaners. They come in a wide range of colors. ◄

225

No room for a home office? Create one in the kitchen or any area with a wall available for installing a desk, shelves, and a few cabinets. Choose colors and materials that coordinate with the rest of the room.

226

Maximize kitchen storage with cabinets that stretch to the ceiling. Incorporating both solid and window cupboards enables you to display beautiful items and hide utilitarian ones.

227

A red checkerboard floor and cabinets finished with crimson glaze bring vibrance and personality to this kitchen.

228

Built-in appliances—including a refrigerator and freezer covered with the same wood paneling as the cabinets—keep a kitchen looking clean and orderly. ▶

229

Simplicity is crucial in a tight space. Here, beadboard on the walls and ceiling provide a clean backdrop for white cabinets—designed to mimic the window—and drawers. Even the dishes are white, adding to the light, airy look.

Enclosing a small kitchen with an open shelving system makes everything easily accessible. Here, covered niches below eye level provide space for odds and ends such as timers, spoon rests, and salt and pepper mills.

231

Pietra Cardosa, a type of schist used here on the countertops and backsplash, offers the beauty of soapstone but is harder and more resistant to scratches. Somewhat porous, this stone should be sealed a few times a year.

232

Wouldn't it be nice if you didn't have to display the mixer, toaster, or knife block, let alone take up precious counter space with them? A kitchen catchall and workspace like the one here lets you conceal those items—and myriad others—but still keep them at your fingertips.

233

You don't need a whole room to devote to a library. Floor-to-ceiling shelving can transform even a small space, such as this alcove, into a cozy spot for books. Adjustable shelves are convenient for stowing volumes of different sizes, and good lighting is key.

234

A built-in bead-board bench topped with a cushion provides a great perch for removing shoes in a mudroom. Add hooks for bags and umbrellas and open shelves with baskets for smaller items. ▶

235

Metal lockers and plenty of hooks help organize miscellaneous items in a garage so that you can easily find what you're looking for. ▶▶

236

Consider applying an epoxy floor coating over concrete in a garage. This creates a shiny surface that is stronger— and more attractive— than concrete alone and is easier to clean. ▶▶

furnishings

237

You might not think to put a loveseat in a hallway unless you knew how invigorating a pop of bright upholstery could be there. This antique piece is newly covered in a vibrant stripe.

238

The main ingredient for a comfy living room? A sofa—or two—you can sink into. These overstuffed, pillow-laden ones fill the bill. Fuzzy tables (that almost resemble lapdogs!) enhance the luxurious, welcoming vibe. ▶

239

Here's a clever idea: convert a beautiful salvage window into a coffee tabletop, as was done in this room with a nineteenth-century Indian wood-and-glass piece. ▶

240

Create a cohesive yet eclectic look by upholstering furnishings in variations on the same hue. The palette in a collection of pear prints inspired the green and brown pieces, including a two-tone sofa, in this room. Notice how different the two armchairs appear—one in lime, the other in forest green. ◄

241

With a throw casually draped over the top, this upholstered coffee table is treated like a sofa or chair, giving the room a warm, easeful quality. ◄

242

Small, easy-to-move rattan pieces make it easy to rearrange a living room for work or socializing.

243

A pair of vintage leather wing chairs, each with its own reading lamp, brings the cozy feeling of a den to a crisp white parlor. ◄

244

Instead of the traditional sofa-armchair-coffee table scenario, consider pulling a dining table up to a banquette in a living room. This offers a more functional space for conversing, working, or casual dining.

245

A dual-purpose room, such as this living and dining space, calls for dual-purpose pieces. These patterned furnishings are pretty enough to display in an elegant setting, and the chairs comfortable enough to pull out for extra seating in the living area.

246

To encourage conversation in a dining space, opt for a round table and sumptuous chairs like these upholstered in a mohair-velvet fabric. A low table arrangement ensures everyone can make eye contact.

247

A dining room doesn't
have to house a dining
set. Mixing stained and
painted pieces, such as this
nineteenth-century walnut
table and whitewashed
chairs from the same
period, looks chic. ◀

248

Garden furniture looks
beautiful in almost any
sunny, casual spot, whether
indoors or out. In this
breakfast nook, scrolled
French benches flank an
antique farm trestle table.

249

If you have small children or otherwise expect furnishings to endure a lot of wear and tear, durable, easy-to-clean cotton or synthetic upholstery is your best bet. Patterned fabrics, such as this plaid, tend to hide stains better than solid cloths.

250

Consider having a new piece professionally aged to match older furnishings. This reproduction dining table was treated so that it would have the same worn, mellow sensibility as the 1920s lyre-back chairs that surround it. ▶

251

If you have a large family
to entertain, consider
setting up a seating area at
one end of an open kitchen.
This gives people a place
to gather apart from the
workspace, while allowing
the cook to socialize. ◄

252

In a small apartment
kitchen, a round table on
wheels can be pulled up
to a built-in bench for
dining or pulled over to the
counter for extra prep space.

253

Rattan furniture—here paired with splashy floral prints—lends a warm, tropical vibe to any kind of room. To keep the pieces looking great, vacuum regularly, as dust accumulates in the textured surfaces. ◄

254

Let the style of a room spill out into a hallway. Here, soft green upholstery and a playfully patterned pillow connect a sophisticated settee, flanked by a Victorian marble-topped table, to the child's room next door.

255

Sometimes a couple of gorgeous pieces in a captivating color are all a room requires. Such is the case in this guest bedroom, where vintage carved wooden beds painted an electrifying blue take center stage.

256

Instead of a chest or bench, consider installing a comfortable sofa at the foot of a bed. Placing small bureaus as bedside tables is another unexpected touch—think of all the storage you'll gain. ▶

257

For an attractive yet functional display on open shelves, store odds and ends in handsome boxes, such as these rattan ones, and keep magazines in vertical files. Scatter a few decorative items throughout and—voilà!

258

Design a bedroom that strikes a pleasing balance between plush and rustic with dramatic, floor-grazing fabrics in homey prints, such as plaids and florals. ▶

259

A canopy bed can be just as beautiful without a canopy. This bed's slender skeleton harmonizes wonderfully with the lines on an antique bamboo desk chair and armoire.

260

Constructed around a
window, built-in closets,
drawers, and open shelves
along one wall of a bedroom
create generous storage,
improve the proportions of
the long, narrow room, and
form the foundation of a
small window seat.

261

Plentiful furnishings in dark and medium hues (navy blue, honey brown) help ground a room with a pale, sweeping ceiling, as illustrated in this photo of a pool house's vaulted, post-and-beam ceiling.

soft touches

262

A crisp paneled tablecloth, in keeping with the formality of an entrance hall, offers a shot of color—and, beneath its skirt, a spot to stow shoes.

263

Instead of fulfilling a practical purpose, curtains can sometimes be used simply to frame a spectacular view. ◄

264

You might not think to pair an Oriental rug with sunny, plaid curtains or a warm red, tan, and gold palette with a watery landscape, but the contrast works beautifully in this room. ◄

265

A couple of alpaca throws warms a bleached palette that includes a sofa and chairs covered in easy-to-care-for muslin slipcovers and pale linen pillows.

266

One way to create an inviting, indulgent space: soften the edges. Here, gracefully gathered shades, a fabric-draped ottoman, skirted upholstery, and a dimpled banquette topped with a multitude of pillows all work to that effect. ◄

267

Linen slipcovers are a smart choice for dining chairs since, unlike upholstery, they can be removed and washed after a spill. It's worth investing in custom covers, as ready-made ones tend to be ill fitting, especially on unusually shaped furniture.

268

For a laid-back look, choose billowy, unlined curtains—which tend to filter light rather than block it—in a cheerful print like this sunny stripe. Go for sleek hardware and avoid fussy valances and swags.

269

Give classic, ladder-back chairs feminine flair with pretty skirted covers. A printed-fabric valance and lampshades provide contrast while continuing the ladylike theme.

270

Here are two things you
don't see very often in
a kitchen: throw pillows
and an elegantly draped
patterned valance. But
in this refined space,
with its window seat and
shiny marble countertops,
they are perfectly
appropriate. ◄

271

Gathered check curtains,
which offer a subtle
counterpoint to ornately
patterned backsplash tiles,
soften glass-front kitchen
cabinets and tie them
into the color scheme.

272

A window seat with an extra-thick cushion makes a cozy spot for napping in a study. If your space doesn't have or permit a seat like this, consider a daybed. ◀

273

The remnants pile at the fabric store is a great place to look for beautiful, inexpensive cloths that are often just the right size for pillows. The ones shown here were all made with fabric scraps.

274

A scenic print, such as a toile, can work wonderfully with a geometric motif like a plaid or stripe. Try letting one pattern dominate, as the toile does here, and allow the other to serve as an accent. ◄

275

When drawn closed, bed curtains block early morning light filtering through the window shutters. In this master bedroom, curtains made of warm wool plaid lined with a luxurious silk taffeta check, both from Christopher Hyland, are as functional as they are beautiful.

276

Vary a motif by using one fabric in different ways. On this porch, the same striped cloth that appears on the shades was cut and pieced back together to form another pattern on the throw pillows.

accents

277

A series of framed black-and-white photographs has a contemporary, art gallery edge that contrasts beautifully with warm, weathered wood furniture.

278

For an intriguing tabletop display, compile different items of various sizes that you love. Here, a 1940s mercury glass lamp, vintage vases, and garden urns mingle effortlessly. The goose soaring overhead is a whimsical touch.

279

A mirror (or painting) and a smattering of vases from different eras, such as this creamy art glass one and a pair of colorful nineteenth-century papier-mâché pieces, dress up a simple mantel. Add flowers when you have them, but the vases also look stunning on their own. ▶

280

One stellar object can inspire a whole palette: Here, the blue, gold, and pink in a lusterware pitcher influenced the room's upholstery.

281

Antique stores and flea markets offer myriad exquisitely crafted, formerly utilitarian pieces—painted sleds, textured washboards, metal watering cans—that can be displayed as art.

282
For maximum intimacy, hang a light fixture about three feet above a dining table. This guideline applies even in a soaring space like this breakfast nook.

283
Large antique Chinese pendant lanterns, of the sort more commonly seen in a living or dining area, bring sophistication to a kitchen. In this room, an ebonized table with Chinoiserie details reiterates the motif.

284

Beautiful china doesn't
have to be kept behind
glass, only to be brought
out on special occasions.
Arrange pieces—such as this
dazzling French Quimper
collection—on open
shelving so they brighten
every meal. ◄

285

Collectibles, such as
delicately painted teapots,
become even more
compelling when displayed
together. Turned to the
side, the rows of spouts
form pleasing silhouettes.

286

When it comes to collecting, there are a few schools of thought. You can go after a certain style, such as the vibrant majolica displayed on an antique étagère in this kitchen . . . ◄

287

. . . or you might amass miscellaneous pieces in a favorite hue, like the cherry-red seen here. To emphasize the theme, these shelves are painted a glossy scarlet.

288

Displayed out of context, in a bedroom or living area, a china collection takes on a grand, artistic sensibility. Here, blue-and-white dishes dotting plate rails in a garret are wonderfully unexpected. ◄

289

Night tables needn't be identical. Here, different tables make the room less formal, while matching lamps establish a sense of balance.

290

A series of miniature compositions can sometimes be as appealing as a single large one. In this bedroom, arrangements of botanical prints and starburst mirrors are hung over the bed and night tables.

291

Ceramic garden stools, like these Chinese antiques, are wonderfully versatile in a sunroom or other living area. Use them as footstools, tables, waterproof plant stands, or extra seating at a party (keep some cushions handy).

292

If you collect items in a favorite color, you will always be able to put together a coordinated, striking display. ▶

outdoors

293

The most important
ingredient needed to create
a relaxing ambiance? Good
lighting. Experiment with a
mix of electric lighting and
candlelight, such as the
sconces (which don't need
to match) and hurricane
lamps seen here—until
you find the right mood.

294

Make a long, narrow terrace
feel cozy by setting up several
different seating areas—here
one for dining and another
for relaxing. ▶

295

A pergola furnished with a built-in grill, countertops, and cabinets (these are covered with gorgeous old cypress shutters) becomes a practical—and magical—outdoor kitchen.

296

An open-air pool house has
the feeling of a cozy living
room when appointed with
indoor-style furnishings,
including oversize floral
pillows that were inspired
by hydrangeas in the garden
(now on the table).

297

Teak furniture and weather-proof acrylic upholstery—almost indistinguishable from cotton canvas—will weather nicely in the elements.

298

Define an outdoor seating area, and protect it from the elements, with curtains made of a heavy, durable material such as cotton duck (shown) or canvas. Contrasting trim makes the utilitarian fabric look decorative.

299

Giant terra-cotta pots filled with fruiting trees, herbs, and flowering plants in staggered sizes infuse a patio or courtyard with color and texture. ◄

300

Bring beautiful patterns and a lovely aroma to a patio by planting greens such as sweet alyssum and creeping thyme between stones. This also contributes to a more natural look, since plants tend to sprout in these spots anyway.

301

An elegant gated arbor—
here punctuating a fence
draped with pink 'Sally
Holmes' roses and bordered
with purple larkspur—
provides a focal point at
the end of a garden path
and a frame for a stunning
view. ◂◂

302

Design a garden with the
sensibility of an Impressionist
painting by planting blooms
such as irises en masse
and letting wildflowers
(buttercups, daisies) grow
as they please. Viewed
from a distance, the colors
blend into magnificent
pastel swaths. ◂

303

On a large property, create
a glorious patchwork by
planting swaths of tall,
unfussy grasses and flowers,
such as purple asters and
feathery, silvery pink
Miscanthus 'Flamingo.'

CHAPTER 5

details

The phrase "God is in the details" is frequently attributed to Le Corbusier, one of the most influential architects in modern history. Consider a shiny row of decorative nail heads marching along the top of a camelback sofa, or the delicate tassels dangling from a curtain panel to understand immediately the big impact small touches can have. As you'll discover in this section, attention to particulars involves more than just choosing beautiful items. It's also about layering patterns and textures, and taking the time to upgrade those less-than-perfect pieces—whether re-covering pillows in gorgeous antique fabric or defining the edge of a cushion with silky fringe. You'll find some grand, yet still exquisitely refined, gestures here, too, such as the handpainted mural on page 293 and the embossed leather wall panels on page 300.

surfaces

304

Who says doors can't be both utilitarian and decorative? A beautifully carved and stained set— Asian-inspired here—is practically a work of art.

305

Anchor a vignette of dishes, such as these bone china pieces, by setting one in a plate stand atop a gilded bracket. Mount the others with plate hangers so that they appear to float around it. ▶

306

Create a sense of light and shadows on a wall by layering yellow-ochre paint over a browner hue. The glow from a candle bulb sconce, like the one made of forged iron here, heightens the blended effect. ▶▶

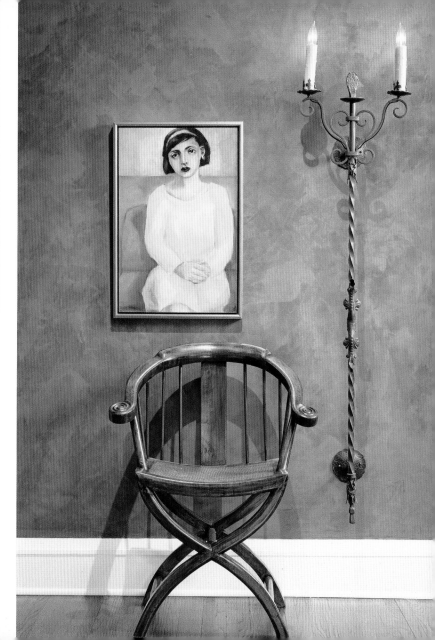

307

Distressed paint and beams made from salvaged timber infuse a living room with old-world appeal. ◄

308

Instead of hanging a painting on the wall, consider painting the wall itself with a beautiful mural. Look for a local artist whose work you admire and ask if he or she will work on commission.

309

Borrow a trick from the
upholstery world and
tack the edges of a piece
of fabric to a wall using
close-set decorative nails.
Enhance the elegant,
custom look with curtains,
seat covers, or a tablecloth
in a matching print.

310

With their minute imperfections, hand-painted walls like these striped ones tend to have a friendlier feel than those dressed with wallpaper. Even stenciled designs can have a similar effect.

311

Intricately carved legs that mimic those on a nearby island lend an exquisite, furniture-like quality to a kitchen sink. Elegant hardware and a slim marble backsplash augment the refined feeling.

312

A marble checkerboard on a backsplash provides a graphic canvas for displaying shiny pots and pans, dishes, and utensils. ▶

313

A marble-topped table that extends from a kitchen island offers informal dining space and extra prep area when needed. ▶

314

A backsplash consisting of mosaic tiles arranged not randomly but in sleek stripes brings a tailored touch to a kitchen. A decorative arch over the range hood frames the motif.

315

Design a dynamic home office using a palette of brown. The key is to contrast textures—the grasscloth walls behind Shoji screens in this scenario—as well as colors. Note the lively combination of dark walnut and pale pine on the desk. ▶

316

The ultimate luxurious wall covering? Warm, leather panels, like those in this library. The embossed damask pattern, which echoes that on an armchair, along with other fine details in the room—silky tassels, decorative nails—add to the feeling of indulgence. ◄

317

Envelop a den, or other cozy space, with softness by covering the walls with rich, velvet fabric. For extra polish, this vibrant cloth is finished with grosgrain ribbon trimmed with decorative nails.

318

Sometimes one wall treatment just won't do— you need three. In this bedroom, molding, hand-stenciled wallpaper, and a swath of bright pink linen are a charming combination.

319

Many retailers reproduce antique wallpaper—such as this chrysanthemum pattern—making it easy and affordable to give a room a pedigreed look. A pair of bright, modern pillows provides contrast. ▶

320

Give a room gorgeous architectural detail by layering latticework panels over walls painted a soft, pastel shade. This is perfect for a sunroom, where the lattice can add to a larger garden theme.

furnishings

321

For a light, airy look, choose sofas and chairs with exposed legs, as opposed to skirted styles. Be sure to consider how the supports will work together with other pieces in the room. Here, claw feet contrast nicely with the angular lines of the coffee tables.

322

Think of upholstery trimmings as the jewelry that completes a beautiful outfit. Notice, for example, how decorative nails highlight the graceful curves of a Louis XV settee and how the thick, textured cord defines the cushion. ◄

323

A muted color scheme and a discreet use of pattern keep the focus on the details, such as the lavender French stitching of these linen-slipcovered Dessin Fournir sofas.

324

Update a pair of armchairs by upholstering the frames in beige raffia and covering the seat cushions with pale blue mohair. As a finishing touch, trim the backs and arms with double rows of nailheads.

325

Mix warm and cool tones in unexpected ways: here, the walls are painted a soft cocoa brown, while the ceiling and the backs of the built-in bookshelves are a pale robin's egg blue.

326

Upholstery nails can be used in a variety of ways—positioned with no gaps between them, known as "close-nailing"; spaced slightly apart; or arranged in parallel rows, referred to as "double-" or "triple-nailing." For a lavishly embellished look, choose pieces, such as this sofa, that combine several techniques.

327

Neutral hues enable solid-, striped-, and floral-upholstered furnishings to mingle effortlessly. Pencil-thin piping on each piece also helps unite them. ▶

328

Trimmings can be used for more than defining edges. This silk braid was sewn onto the face of a slipper chair, creating a delicate patterned border. Solid-hued piping provides the chair a crisp outline.

329

Paintings don't have to reside on walls: This hand-painted lattice-arabesque motif turns a television cabinet into an elaborate showpiece.

soft touches

330

Silk balloon shades edged with a thick band of braid have the look of an elegant ball gown. In fact, in seventeenth-century Europe, when such trimmings were first used, the same kinds of ornaments that adorned upholstery also graced women's dresses.

331

An elegant space often calls for curtains, but when they are not feasible, as with a very narrow window, a structured fabric pelmet—this one is finished with contrasting braid—strikes just the right note.

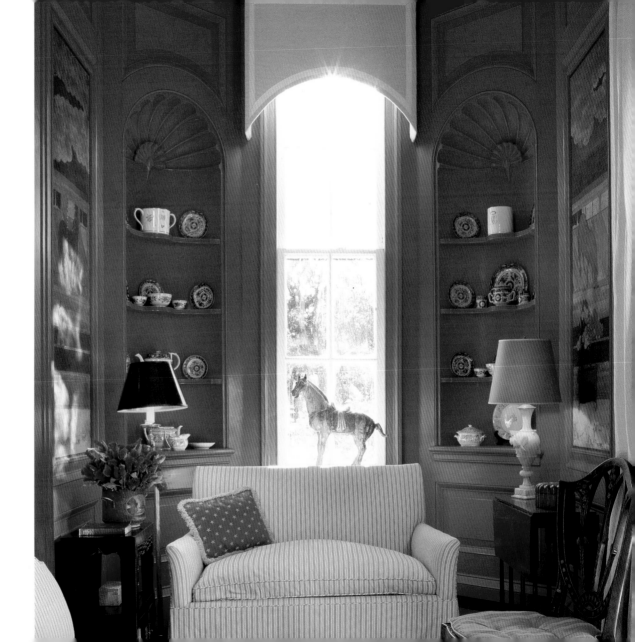

332

Who knew felt could be so glamorous? Used to make the bands, loops, and fleur-de-lis that trim these lofty curtains, the fuzzy fabric complements the weight of the wool-silk panels and proves to be an elegant ornament indeed. ◄

333

A boldly patterned rug that stretches almost the length of a room helps to define the color palette and unite different seating groups in a sweeping space. ◄

334

Bands of checked fabric temper the formality of ivory pleated curtains. The country-style chandelier hung over the graceful table surrounded with Louis XIV–inspired chairs has a similar effect.

335

Encourage lingering over a meal by treating a breakfast nook banquette as if it were a sofa and piling on the pillows. A lazy Susan placed in the center of the table makes serving a breeze.

336

Give vertically striped curtains extra edge by finishing the leading sides with folded bands of the same fabric, turned horizontally.

337

The pattern play continues at the dining table in this room: note how unexpected a pair of living room–style wing chairs accented with striped pillows looks mixed with wooden chairs with floral crewelwork seats.

338

A tapestry—such as this English antique—has a neater, more polished look when stretched across panels, and mounted edge-to-edge. Achieve a similar effect with any beautifully patterned fabric. Here, a coverlet made from pieced-together vintage cloths complements the wall hanging.

339

Linen wall fabrics add an extra touch of comfort, coziness, and quiet to a guest bedroom. ▶

340

Sumptuous fabrics
can bring texture to a
monochromatic room.
Here, a sofa, chair, and
ottoman are upholstered
in distressed palomino
leather, promising instant
relaxation to anyone who
pauses for a rest. ◄

341

Create an alluring nook
for a bed by overlapping
different fabrics. In this
space, a toile panel and
overhanging valance frame
shiny satin pillows and a
plush silk-velvet headboard.
Artwork is hung on top of
the curtain, contributing
to the layered look.

342

Checked fabric has a tendency to look homespun—but not when it's gathered into an elaborate sunburst canopy finished with pencil-pleat panels. Matching lampshades and monogrammed linens heighten the sophistication.

343

Create balance in a room with lots of pattern by choosing one of the prints' non-dominant colors—in this case soft lavender— for the walls. ▶

344

A custom duvet cover with a ruffled edge made from the same fabric adds luster to a master bedroom. Window treatments and a decorative pillow cover, also made from the same fabric, keep the look cohesive. ▶

345

Familiar plaids and stripes are among the most comforting patterns. Keep them looking fresh by layering different styles of the same motif, as with the armchair, throw, and window shades in this bedroom.

346

Thick moss fringe, named for the velvety forest covering it resembles, lends a luxurious touch to pillows and cushions. This trimming looks especially appropriate in a nature-themed setting, like this sunroom.

accents

347

Make a grand entrance by outfitting a front door with glamorous accents, such as beveled glass windows, and gracious architectural details, like columns and cornices.

348

For a brilliant display, try arranging colorful glass vases, such as these mid-century ones, so that they overlap on a windowsill. The pieces will look different depending on the direction of the sun, creating a kaleidoscopic effect.

349

Sometimes even clothing can be presented as art. Take this gauzy circa-1800 Chinese undergarment, which is mounted on a pole above a nineteenth-century elm grain chest, also from China.

350

Scour Web sites and online auctions for beautiful antique fabrics you can use for pillows. (The golden ones here were made with luxurious eighteenth-century cloth.) Old pieces have a warmth and personality that new fabric can't match. Just be sure to ask the seller about any holes or stains before making a purchase. ▶

351

Hand-painted tiles turn an unremarkable fireplace into a work of art. These, which feature figurines in various action poses, lend a sense of playfulness and tie into a broader Chinoiserie theme.

352

A grouping of artwork need not be arranged symmetrically. These engravings, which complement the paneled architecture, show how refreshing an unbalanced display can be. ▶

353

Take a traditional item, such as a chandelier, combine it with an unexpected material, like wooden beads (did you ever imagine they could look so elegant?), and you've got a spectacular showpiece.

354

Create a festive spirit at a dinner party by designing a table around a theme. Here, shell- and coral-adorned pieces lend a soft, beachy vibe.

355

The smallest details—
a silk tassel dangling
from a china cabinet key,
openwork embellishment
on a tablecloth, a bright
ribbon cinching a napkin at
a place setting—can make
an elegant space feel even
more gracious.

356

An old-fashioned look doesn't have to be rough-hewn. Pretty Delft tiles (which originated in The Netherlands in the sixteenth century), elaborately carved woodwork, and delicate hardware give a kitchen a classic, sophisticated air.

357

When designing center-pieces, think outside the flower garden (or market). Found items such as berries, branches, leaves, and seedpods can all lend themselves to an intriguing, and unexpected, seasonal display.

358

A playful font and modern plaid fabric offer a welcoming message on a guest bedroom pillow.

359

Update traditional architecture in a bathroom with ultra-modern fixtures—such as this sleek, freestanding faucet—and sophisticated touches like museum-style lighting over a pair of peaceful landscape paintings.

outdoors

360

Brighten a gazebo or covered porch with a frieze. In this photo, a Matisse-inspired motif of frolicking swimmers is painted on interior beams. A graphic wallpaper border would also give the same effect.

361

You can treat outdoor teak furnishings, like this bench and pair of chairs, with a sealer or oil to maintain their original amber color, but why bother? The pieces naturally fade to a silver-gray that is just as beautiful.

362

Add a splash of color to a garden or yard with low-maintenance blooming perennials—such as the *Persicaria* 'Firetail' here.

CHAPTER 6

color

It's not surprising that many people are intimidated when choosing colors. With all the subtle shades and potentially endless combinations available, it may seem hard to know where to start. But nothing sets the tone of a room like color. Red, for example, is so powerful that studies have shown that the mere sight of it can cause one's heart to beat faster, while pink has proven to have a sedative effect. Cool blues tend to create a soothing, calm, and relaxed atmosphere, while neutral colors simply allow the other colors in a room to take center stage. When coming up with a palette, consider not only what mood you want to create, but also the shades that please you. Think about the clothes you like to wear, the artwork you favor, and the places you love to visit. The rich scarlets, oranges, and golds in a favorite painting or the neutral sand and sea shades of the beach can be a launching point for an entire scheme.

surfaces

363

Rich, velvety-red walls make a small formal room feel positively regal (and a china collection pop). Choose a flat paint finish, rather than glossy, which tends to look more racy.

364

When you have a room painted a bold color, keep the palette of adjoining spaces relatively neutral.

365

Another unexpected way to inject color is to paint the steps of a staircase. A runner, here with vibrant stripes, protects the paint from wear.

366

Rooms in an open floor plan don't have to be decorated the same way, but they should coordinate. Here, the bright orange in pairs of striped curtains is just enough to connect the space to the adjoining color-drenched living area. ◄

367

Paint a room an eye-popping shade and you've actually made choosing furnishings easier, since neutrals are often the best bet in this scenario. Tie the look together with a few accents that match the walls, such as the pillow and desk accessories seen here.

368

For a warm, mottled glow—rather than a shock of saturated color—apply golden paint over walls finished with rough plaster. ◄

369

Are you attracted to vivacious hues but wary of using them in an entire room? Consider painting just the ceiling—in this room, a lime green—and balancing it with a sprinkling of bright furnishings and accessories.

370

Life imitating—or mingling with—art can produce a sensational effect. In this dining room, a Chinese ginger jar echoes one in the hand-painted wallpaper, while a delicate sconce looks as though it were part of an illustrated chandelier.

371

Elaborately patterned wallpaper, like this floral print, offers a wealth of shades to choose from when selecting furnishings. In this hallway, pink, green, blue, and gold pieces work beautifully together. ▶

372

Muted metallic wallpaper
is a brilliant choice for
any light-filled space—
even a study. To keep it
from feeling showy, choose
neutral-hued furniture and
rustic accents, such as the
barn star and chandelier
seen here.

373

If you have different types of walls in the same room, consider painting just one kind of surface, as was done with the board-and-batten here. This provides a glorious shot of color (without painting the whole room) and makes the varying architecture seem more deliberate.

374

Give a new living space the homey feeling of a generations-old barn by installing rusticated wood beams and a pair of sliding doors painted a vibrant shade.

375

Think red for a dining room. Here, a wall of bookshelves—painted with high-gloss Chinese red and decorated with eighteenth-century Italian engravings—sets off eighteenth-century silver-gilt armchairs and a round mahogany table. ▶

376

Silvery and white touches—
such as pewter chandeliers,
a large contemporary mirror
with a silver-gilt frame, and
white-painted shutters—set
off the rich blue walls and
secure a fresh mood in this
traditional dining room. ◀

377

For a gorgeous, two-tone
look, install wainscoting
around the perimeter of a
room, and then paint the rest
of the walls and the ceiling
a bright hue. The narrow
band of color provides a
great place to showcase
artwork, as in this room.

378

When your color scheme says one thing—here, cheerful blue-and-white has a French provincial flavor—and your furnishings another—the new dark-wood furnishings look contemporary—you've got an exciting mix. ◄

379

Create a refreshingly bold look in a kitchen by painting not just cabinets, but also their interiors and moldings, with a dazzling shade. Uninterrupted by white space, the color packs a serious punch.

380

Increase the vivaciousness
in a kitchen with a mosaic
tile backsplash made up
of bright yellow, red, and
orange tiles mixed with a
sprinkling of more calming
colors, such as lavender
and olive green.

381

Have you ever dreamed of using three or more colors of paint in one room? You might get tired of these schemes in a living area, but an out of the way spot, such as a laundry room, is a great place to live out a color fantasy.

382

Strié is a streaked design created by dragging a brush through glaze applied over a base color. Thanks to its subtlety, this treatment—here rendered in luminous pale peach—is easy to match with other patterns.

383

Keep cheerful, country-style motifs (checks, quilt patterns) from feeling chintzy by choosing prints in a single fresh shade, such as the spring green seen here. ▶

384

White comes in hundreds of shades—some slightly blue, others more gray, pink, or gold. To find the right one, compare paint chips with the other colors in the room. Here, furnishings painted a warm, apricot-tinged white are a perfect match for tawny walls.

385

Fabrics and wallpaper printed with a classic American buffalo check create a sense of welcome in a guest bedroom. A pale sophisticated color, such as beige, prevents the homespun pattern from appearing kitschy. ▶

386

Colors don't have to
be bright to be effective.
Textured, gray-blue wallpaper
and matching toile linens
turn this bedroom into
a sumptuous escape.

387

A blue shade, such as that in this mosaic tile, is a wonderfully soothing choice for a bathroom. Given the color of the grout, white is a natural accent. Play up the scheme with snowy marble surfaces and a speckled floor that incorporates both hues.

388

White walls and bare windows are anything but dull when juxtaposed with furnishings in rich, saturated colors and varying materials, such as the mohair-velvet sofa and leather-and-wrought iron chairs in this living area.

389

An array of differently upholstered seating can lend an air of sophistication to a living room—if the color palette is limited to few colors, here blue, pink, and green. ▶

390

Color helps make formal furnishings feel more inviting, an effect that is even more pronounced when the pieces are upholstered in soft, tactile materials, such as the blue suede, brown cotton-velvet, and pink velveteen seen here.

391

Enliven a sedate, two-tone palette with a variety of patterns (florals, checks, dots), contrasting trimmings, and other pretty details such as button-tufting or decorative nail heads. ◄

392

Infuse soft hues, such as aqua and pink, with energy by combining them with an arresting pattern. To keep the look consistent, not busy, repeat one motif throughout the room. Here, the diamond design even appears on the carpet.

393

Tomato-red plus sumptuous suede add up to an attention-grabbing piece of furniture. Indeed, a pair of these chairs is all that's needed to invigorate a room. Cocoa-brown suede welt helps define their graceful lines.

394

Think how uninspired this space would feel without the scarlet chenille chairs and door painted to match. The bright shades not only give the viewer a bit of a jolt (often a key component of modern decor), but also infuse the space with warmth and personality. ▶

395

Be adventurous by choosing
an unconventional color
combination for a room.
Here, turquoise blue,
brown, and lime green give
this bedroom a vivacious
personality.

soft touches

396

Floor-length draperies made from a striped tone-on-tone fabric harmonize with shimmery wall covering in a similar hue and reinforce the calming quality of a soft, monochromatic palette in a living room.

397

A vibrant red rug atop a faux
marbleized wood floor helps
ground the space in a two-
story room. Tall curtains in
the same hue as the carpet
create visual unity and
accentuate the scale.

398

Roll out a red carpet and you'll have enough character to keep everything else in the room neutral. Try contrasting the rich shade with an ethereal one that changes color with the light, such as the pale periwinkle seen here on the walls.

399

Pleated plaid chair covers may seem like an outlandish match for Chinoiserie furnishings, but the seats' fresh green shade and feminine style enable them to mingle effortlessly with the room's floral motifs. ◄

400

One foolproof way to create a harmonious palette: work with shades that fall next to each other on the color wheel, such as the soft blues and mauves seen here.

401

Chairs featuring upholstery painted with elegant Chinoiserie scenes are a lovely counterpoint to modern accents, such as this squiggle-pattern rug and simple striped curtains.

402
Cover a set of dining chairs in several different colors of the same fabric for a subtle rainbow effect. Go with a simple pattern and muted hues to keep the look from appearing busy.

403

Cloud-white is a natural accent for linens, shades, and the like. To gaze up at this brilliant gathered canopy is almost like looking into a clear blue sky.

404

For those with color commitment issues, vibrant, patterned pillows, such as the ones in this teen's room, are an ideal solution. Less permanent than paint or upholstery, the cushions can be easily swapped in and out.

405

A built-in reading bench offers extra storage, with four drawers perfect for stowing photos, books, shoes, or whatever else can fit.

406

Give colorful pieces greater
presence in a whitewashed
space by "framing" them
with both hard and soft
edges. In this young girl's
room, an iron daybed
outlines a smattering of
bright pillows, while a Lucite
table subtly delineates a pair
of graphic floor cushions.

407

You can't go wrong with a
palette inspired by natural
surroundings. In this beach
house bedroom, blue-gray
fabrics echo the shade
of the sea on a stormy day
and pale brown recalls
the sand. ◄

408

Fiery orange—a color the
modernist Russian painter
Wassily Kandinsky once
compared to "a church bell,
a strong contralto voice"—
makes a powerful statement
in any space. Temper it with
a cool shade, such as blue,
and notes of white.

409

A room composed of rose, pale lemon, and sky-blue shades has all of the energy a primary color palette imparts but none of the harshness. Mix in patterns for an even livelier look. ◄

410

Gold accents bring sophistication to a bedroom, here by way of the handpainted chest of drawers and three-person bench at the foot of the bed.

411

The pictorial nature of toile makes it an ideal choice for a child's room. Opt for a modern, whimsical print like this red one, rather than a traditional style, which tends to be fancy.

412

Another fresh way to work with color is to choose pieces in different shades of one color. Here, a bed and chaise upholstered in pink velvet are accented with an antique rug and pillows in darker and lighter hues. ▶

413

Some of the most
striking contrasts come
from juxtaposing pieces
in complementary colors,
such as the rosy carpet and
emerald-green fronds in this
sunroom. A smattering of
neutral furnishings ensures
that the combination isn't
overpowering. ◄

414

Create a segue between
rooms by installing doorway
curtains that set the tone
for the space you're about
to enter. Here, a pair of
vibrant tartan panels hints
at the grand yet cheerful
sunroom beyond.

accents

415

Here's an easy recipe for a dynamic color scheme: Choose a graphic abstract painting, then make sure each of its colors is represented at least once on a pillow, chair, vase, or another accent elsewhere in the room. ◄

416

Punctuate a black-and-white palette—made more exciting here by layering different patterns—with pieces in a single bright hue, such as magenta, for a look that exudes modern glamour.

417

Beloved for its cheerful disposition, yellow can also look formal and sophisticated. If it's this muted glow (rather than a ray of sunlight) you're after, look no further than this elegant, golden tableau for inspiration.

418

An organic art glass panel is a beautiful vehicle for reinforcing a palette, such as the spring greens and neutrals seen here. If your taste is more traditional, opt for a less-abstract stained glass piece or perhaps a window salvaged from a church. ▶

419

Let a two-color rug set the color palette for a room. In this living room, everything is a variation of red or light brown. ◄

420

Modern abstract motifs often mimic the natural world, making them an ideal choice in a room with rustic accents. Notice, for example, how the shapes on this vivid rug subtly echo the stones on the fireplace. ◄

421

One way to choose artwork for a neutral space: pick colors that are slightly brighter and have a bit more pigment than those already in the room. Here, straw yellow becomes a canary shade in the painting; tawny brown is translated as orange.

422

Hints of warm brass—on
door handles, drawer pulls,
candlesticks, and decorative
nails—bring soft luster to a
golden palette. To keep the
metal gleaming, dust and
clean occasionally with
dish soap and warm water.
Polish tarnished pieces
when needed. ◄

423

Some vases, like this ornate
Imari pair, are colorful
works of art. Let them shine
by filling them with simple,
unfussy flowers. Branches or
foliage would also be a nice
complement.

424

Classic blue-and-white dishware looks fresh when displayed not just in a china cabinet but also on walls, ledges, and sideboards. Here, the eclectic presentation suits the casual vibe of a rustic dining space. ◀

425

Decoupage pieces—such as the colorful plates displayed here—can look surprisingly elegant, despite the humble materials (paper cutouts, varnish) used to create them.

426

Fresh flowers or fresh fruit can add a splash of color in a breakfast nook featuring neutral colors.

427

Small appliances—such as toasters, mixers, and beverage refrigerators like this one—now come in a rainbow of shades and offer a great opportunity to incorporate splashes of color into a kitchen. ◄◄

428

For a chic party look, mix up a signature cocktail that tastes delicious *and* enhances the decor. This cranberry-guava drink, arranged on a lime-green tray, adds welcome bursts of bright color to a summertime fete. ◄

429

Bring a whimsical touch to a snowy kitchen by painting stools in pretty pastel hues. Pinches of the same shades sprinkled throughout the room create a cohesive scheme.

430
Keep a red-and-green scheme from feeling one-note (or evocative of the holidays) by mixing patterns and integrating a wide range of shades, such as forest, lime, cherry, and cotton candy.

431

Bring extra cheer to the sunporch of a beach house by painting the walls and ceiling the same shade of sea green.

432

Keep an eclectic collection of wicker sunporch furniture from feeling too mismatched by using the same color palette for all of the cushions.

outdoors

433

Brighten a collection of
rattan furniture with a few
coats of glossy spray paint.
These items are upholstered
with pieces cut from a
vibrant, striped rug.

434

An outdoor space needn't be permanent. In this photo, an Indian wedding tent and some cast-off pillows define an appealing outdoor room. Commingling in a riot of color and patterns, the fabrics include everything from French country to Balinese designs.

435

Instead of planting a garden alongside a house, consider arranging pots of all shapes, colors, and sizes filled with lush blooms. The planters add texture and can be easily swapped in and out. For a coordinated look, choose flowers in variations on the same hue, such as pinks and oranges.

436

A lush blanket of ivy, which is hardy and easy to care for, brings glorious color to the facade of a house. Punctuate the emerald expanse with bright, contrasting shutters. Ivy is also a great solution for an unsightly wall. ▶

437

Set against an alabaster backdrop, bright blue outdoor accents can magnify the brilliance of the sky. Together, the colors recall the whitewashed buildings topped with azure church domes that populate the Greek islands.

438

Faux bois furniture, made from a concrete-like resin shaped to look like twisted tree branches, can be a fitting accent in a garden. Update the style, which was invented in nineteenth-century France, with bright cushions.

439

Highlight a row of majestic-yet-unassuming trees, such as these scarlet oaks, with a shock of bright orange daylilies. The blooms require little maintenance beyond cutting them back in the fall.

440

A simple, unfinished redwood arbor bordered by a tall hedge and dotted with an abundance of pink 'Zephrine Drouhin' roses creates a colorful entry to a garden. ▶

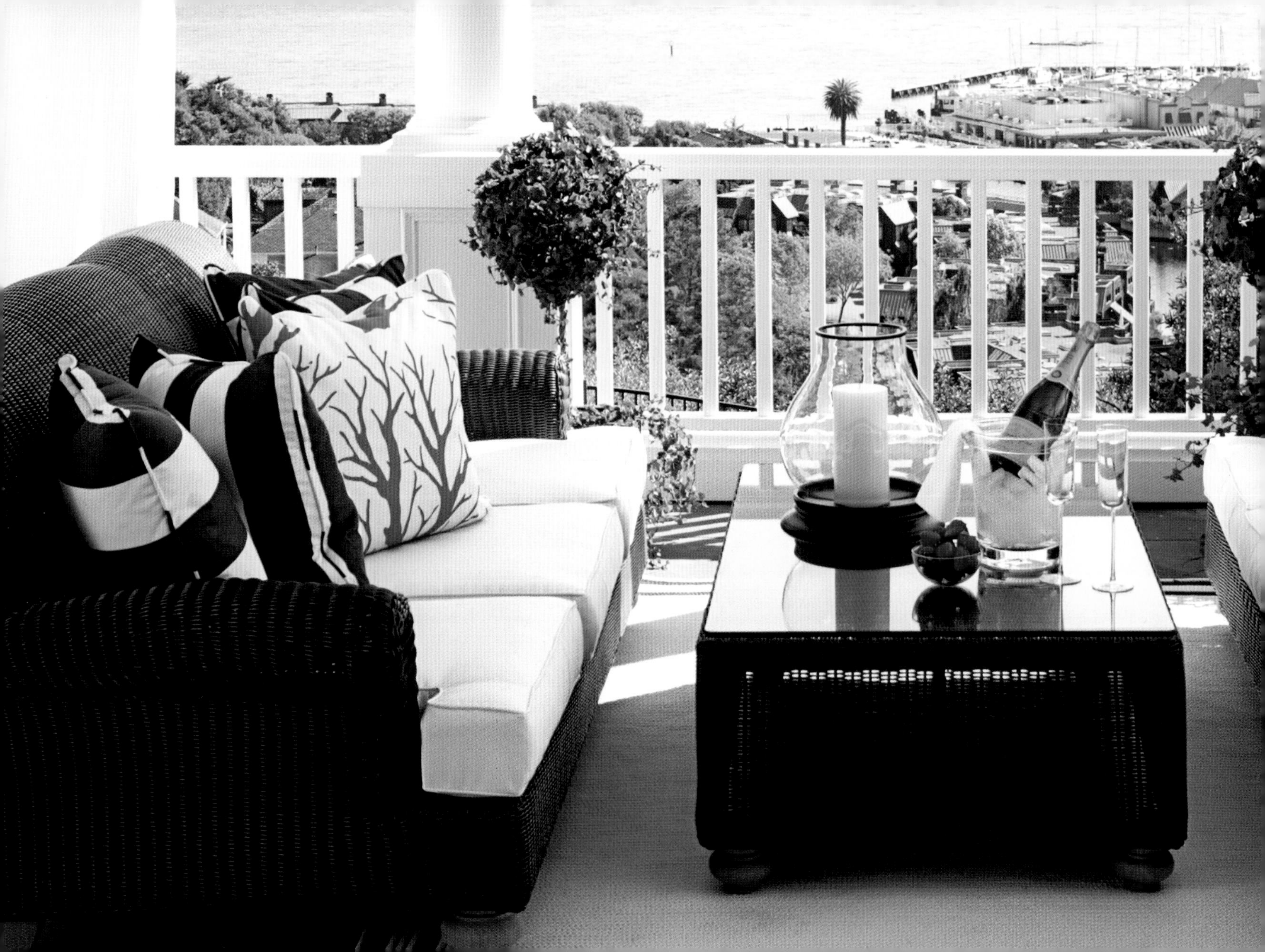

CHAPTER 7

quick fixes

So you'd like to revitalize a room (or two) but not in the radical way often seen on television makeover shows. Let's just say you don't see yourself hiring a demolition crew, or even an interior designer, anytime soon. That's where the quick fix comes in—that relatively small but oh-so-satisfying upgrade you can do in a few days, a few hours, maybe even a few minutes. Whether it's applying a fresh coat of paint to the walls, replacing a window frame, finding the perfect spot for a flea market find, arranging potted plants around a doorway, or tying colorful cushions onto dark-colored chairs, you can easily put a new spin on a tired look. The change may not be dramatic, but you'll find the results gratifying nonetheless.

surfaces

441

Enliven any space by painting the walls and ceiling two different hues, like the spicy paprika and saffron seen here. ◄

442

It's amazing what a fresh coat of paint can do. Here, sky blue walls make white cotton chair covers, Murano glass chandeliers, and other furnishings seem brighter, their edges crisper.

443

Paint the back of a cabinet an electifying shade—such as the red shown here— and make a beautiful china service really pop. You can achieve a similar look with wallpaper. ◂◂

444

For a touch of color in a neutral space, try painting just a window or doorframe, which is less expected (and less work) than painting an entire room. Note in this photo how the mint green breaks up the repetitiveness of the paneling in this kitchen. ◂

445

Look for unconventional wall coverings. In this top-floor study, a map of the world was affixed like wallpaper to a canted wall. Framed maps on an adjoining wall echo the theme.

446

Instead of refinishing worn wood floors with polyurethane, consider painting them with bold stripes. The motif makes a room appear wider and grander, and can serve as a foundation for other patterns and colorful furnishings.

447

Mirrors—or in this case mirrored paneling in the fireplace and on a sconce—and whitewashed surfaces keep a cramped room with tiny windows from feeling too small or dark. ▶

448

Try juxtaposing not just
paint colors but finishes too.
Here, white semigloss (the
ideal finish for a bathroom)
is used on the wainscoting
and ceiling, while the rest
of the walls are treated
with soothing gray in a
matte finish.

449

A sunroom with a ceiling covered in luminous silver leaf, a thin foil, positively glows. Purchase silver (or gold) leaf in rolls and apply it yourself, or hire a painter who specializes in decorative techniques to do the work. You can also get a similar effect with silver or gold paint.

furnishings

450

If you entertain often, consider housing liquor and bar equipment in a beautiful armoire in the living room. A wall-mounted shelf can hold glasses. ◄

451

Refresh a tired or outdated sofa with new upholstery in a neutral color that won't go out of style, such as white. Change the look by rotating pillows with the seasons: pale cotton in summertime, dark-colored velvet in winter, and so on. ◄

452

Here's a simple way to customize a cushioned chair or stool: cover the top with a piece of canvas decorated with pretty grosgrain ribbon in varying widths and colors.

453

When painting furniture you use often, such as a dining table, choose a high-gloss product and top with several coats of a clear protective finish to guard against scratches, dings, and discoloration.

454

Revive flea-market chairs with white paint and fresh fabric, such as this vibrant Chinese print. You can do the upholstering yourself: just remove the seats, cut fabric to size, and affix with a staple gun.

455

An easy alternative to upholstering is to purchase seat cushions, which can instantly brighten dark chairs—like the vintage metal ones in this photo—or hide flaws on flea-market finds.

456

Eliminate clutter in a home office by storing everything from stationery to knitting needles in wicker baskets that can be easily tucked into bookshelves.

457

For a distinctive, pattern-on-pattern look, cover the back of a china cabinet with wallpaper that coordinates with, but doesn't match, that on the walls. The toile used here reinforces the room's red-and-white scheme and highlights a collection of antique dishes.

458

Here's an ingenious way to disguise a flat-screen TV. The custom-upholstered bench shown here has a detachable top. Remove the top and the screen pops up with the press of a button on a remote control. ▶

459

Transform beautiful found doors—here from Mexico—into decorative screens. Connect two or more panels with hinges and, if you like, replace panes with mirrors, as was done here. The pieces would also look pretty with their original glass.

460

Keep a small guest bedroom feeling airy and light by leaving canopy beds bare. Embellish them with small flourishes, such as the silver gilt finials seen here atop Colonial-style beds. ▶

461

Give a garret guest bedroom a romantic air with a vintage metal-frame bed. In this room, the color of an old bench with chipped paint—placed at the foot of the bed—inspired the hues of lampshades, rugs, and blankets.

462

Create a dramatic, three-dimensional headboard in a snap by arranging a row of tall white shutters behind a bed. Use the same shutters on windows for a cohesive look. ▶

463

Wicker furniture brings wonderful texture to casual decor. The pieces typically come in white or natural shades, but you can change them to any color you like with a few coats of glossy spray paint. ▶

soft touches

464

Define rooms—
without closing them
off completely—with a
dramatic sweep of fabric
drawn to one side. This
striped silk curtain is
mounted on a rod above
an arched doorway and
tied back with cord.

465

Convert a pair of pleated curtains into canopies for twin beds. To make them, two corbels were painted white and twenty-one eyehooks were screwed, evenly spaced, around their flat edges. The corbels were then mounted to the wall above the bed with heavy-duty picture hangers, graded for at least one hundred pounds. Curtain pins attached to each pleat were then hooked into the corbels' eyehooks.

466

Consider hanging tab-top curtains around the perimeter of a canopy bed. You can enshroud the bed entirely or install panels only at the back, creating a gauzy headboard.

467

Hang curtains outside a window seat. They can be pulled closed for privacy indoors.

468

Create a luxe, romantic look in a bedroom with curtains, bed hangings, a dust ruffle, and tablecloth that all graze or pool on the floor. ▶

469

An antique kimono was used to create this extra-long bolster pillow, but you could create a similar effect with a beautiful piece of silk. Drape another swath of silk over a canopy bed or tie the fabric to the poles of a four-poster bed.

470

An Oriental rug, typically a living room mainstay, looks fresh in a bedroom. Even though these carpets are made of durable wool, you should vacuum them regularly to remove dirt that can break down the yarn fibers.

471

Bring softness and pattern to a bathroom vanity or sink area by replacing cabinet doors with a gathered fabric skirt. You could also dress up a freestanding vanity this way.

472

A vintage pull-work tablecloth is easy to transform into a charming shower curtain. Topstitched to the back of the tablecloth, a piece of lime-green fabric, with raw edges pressed in, provides a contrasting backing. Buttonholes along the top (made with a sewing machine) hold decorative hooks, which also support a plastic liner.

accents

473

Customize a plain wreath to coordinate with your existing decor—in this case the ribbons on (and suspending) the wreath match the beige linen curtains lined with sage check fabric.

474

Give items displayed on shelves room to breathe so that you can truly enjoy each one. If you have a large collection and little space, rotate pieces in and out every so often.

475

Canvases presented
without frames have a
three-dimensional effect.
Set against a white
background, the birds
in these paintings appear
to be in flight. ◀

476

You may need to improvise
a bit when hanging an
odd number of prints,
such as these nine vintage
photographs. Here, the
pictures are mounted not
just above a credenza, but
also over a chair; one print
is dropped down to fill the
gap between the furniture,
creating a pleasing,
balanced look.

477

A few pieces of Native American pottery bring rich color and intriguing forms to a small mantel. ◄◄

478

Add interest to a bare wall by mounting a vintage bracket upside down and using it to display a small collection— here of shells, sand dollars, and starfish. ◄

479

Spruce up a wall by gathering beautiful platters or other dishes at a flea market and then mounting them with plate hangers. Before hanging them, experiment with different configurations by making paper cutouts of the pieces and arranging them on the wall with painter's tape.

480

Easier than dividing one
large map into framed
sections (but just as
spectacular), you can
purchase a series of maps,
frame them, and mount
them en masse. This
floor-to-ceiling display of
sand-colored plats depicts
Miami Beach in 1943. ◀

481

Keep proportion in mind
when playing with shapes in
a room. Here, the generous
size of a round mirror makes
it work with an armless sofa's
boxy silhouette. A circular
table and trio of glass orbs
echo the mirror's form.

482

Create a compelling tableau with a collection of similar artwork (here French landscapes) by hanging some items and propping up others in stands or against a wall.

483

A smattering of playful pieces—a fluorescent beach ball painting; bright, geometric-pattern vases; an oblong pendant lamp— keep the mood in a modern dining space light and fun. ▶

484

One quirky piece, like this monkey-shape planter, and a lively yellow accent breathe new life into a contemporary kitchen—and reveal the owners' fun-loving sense of humor.

485

Considered a good-luck symbol, metal or wood barn stars—used to decorate barns in the eighteenth and nineteenth centuries—are often found at flea markets and antiques shops. The pieces have a cheerful, rustic quality that is just right for a kitchen.

486

Sometimes a display can be both decorative and functional. Arranging a beautiful collection of dishes, such as this cheerful Cornish Ware, on open shelves is a great way to address both needs. ◄

487

An American flag makes a strong statement indoors. This giant, vintage flag sets a bright color palette for a children's room.

488

Simple, practical items—
a warm teak tray for holding
toiletries, a pretty carved
soap dish, an array of artful
sea sponges—bring natural
beauty to a bathroom.

489

Plants of all shapes
and sizes—along with
accessories such as floral
pillows and a mirror frame
crafted from twigs—help
connect a screened-in
porch to the outdoors.

outdoors

490

Few color schemes pack more of a punch than black and white accented with a single vibrant hue, such as the coral seen on the patterned throw pillows in this breezy outdoor space. ◄

491

When it comes to creating a sumptuous, inviting look, you can't have too many pillows. On this covered porch, pillows of all shapes and sizes in bright cottons and silks make a wrought-iron daybed an ideal spot to curl up for a nap.

492

Design a vibrant, semi-private outdoor shower stall by adding grommets to a pair of canvas panels, then threading ropes through and hanging the cloths from rods mounted overhead.

493

Let teak furniture weather naturally so that it effortlessly blends into its outdoor surroundings.

494

Beautiful containers, such as a handcrafted basket or vintage pot embellished with a mosaic, can make even familiar plants like petunias or marigolds feel distinctive.

495

Stationary sheer fabric panels soften sunlight without blocking views from a semi-enclosed outdoor space. They can be gathered with rope or twine for easy access to the surrounding gardens.

496

If you don't have room or time for a garden, you can still create a lush look by arranging planters around a doorway and letting vines like honeysuckle grow over a railing or fence. ▶

497

A swing made of fragrant, weather-resistant cedar, left in its natural color and finished with a clear stain, is extremely low maintenance. Dress it up with colorful pillows. ◄

498

Restore an old, chipped porch swing with a fresh coat of color: Scrape off loose paint and lightly sand. Prime, paint, and finish with a clear protective topcoat.

499

A brick house can be painted any color. A coat of pastel pink paint, tempered by warm gray shutters and white trim, gives the old-world material a dreamy, romantic air. ◄

500

A teak table, seen here with Adirondack chairs that blend with the verdant landscape, is an ideal choice for an outdoor spot. The wood's high oil content makes it water- and rot-resistant so you can leave it out year round.

photography credits

Page 2: John Gould Bessler
Page 5: Oberto Gili
Pages 6–7: Karyn R. Millet
Page 9: Eric Piasecki
Pages 10–11: John Gould Bessler
Page 12: William Waldron
Page 13: Michel Arnaud
Page 14: Tria Giovan
Page 15: Carlos Emilio
Page 16: Tria Giovan
Page 17: Ellen McDermott
Page 18: Grey Crawford
Page 19: Laura Moss
Page 20: Roger Davies
Page 21: Pieter Estersohn
Page 22: Tim Street-Porter
Page 23: Edmund Barr
Page 24: Pieter Estersohn
Page 25: Erik Kvalsvik
Page 26: Gordon Beall
Page 27: Gordon Beall
Page 28: Fritz von der Schulenburg
Page 29: Eric Piasecki
Page 30: Tria Giovan
Page 31: Simon Upton
Page 32 (left): Simon Upton
Page 32 (right): Tim Street-Porter
Page 33: Grey Crawford
Page 34: John Gould Bessler
Page 35: Antoine Bootz
Page 36: Eric Piasecki
Page 37: Tria Giovan
Page 38: Laura Moss
Page 39: Frances Janisch
Page 40: Tim Street-Porter
Page 41: Tim Street-Porter
Page 42: Frances Janisch
Page 43: Eric Piasecki

Page 44 (left): Eric Piasecki
Page 44 (right): Dominique Vorillon
Page 45: Jeff McNamara
Page 46: Gordon Beall
Page 47: John Gould Bessler
Page 48: Ellen McDermott
Page 49: Kerri McCaffety
Page 50: Susan Gilmore
Page 51: Eric Piasecki
Page 52: Frances Janisch
Page 53: Jeremy Samuelson
Page 54: Oberto Gili
Page 55: Tim Street-Porter
Page 56: Dominique Vorillon
Page 57: Dominique Vorillon
Page 58: Eric Piasecki
Page 59: John Gould Bessler
Page 60: John Gould Bessler
Page 61: Pieter Estersohn
Page 62: Simon Upton
Page 63: Chuck Baker
Page 64: Nina Bramhall
Page 65: Vivian Russell
Page 66: Nina Bramhall
Page 67: John M. Hall
Pages 68–69: Laura Resen
Page 70: Jack Thompson
Page 71: John Gould Bessler
Page 72: Grey Crawford
Page 73: Ken Hayden
Page 74: Roger Davies
Page 75: John M. Hall
Page 76: Simon Upton
Page 77: John Gould Bessler
Page 78: Tria Giovan
Page 79: Ellen McDermott
Page 80: Peter Murdock
Page 81: Peter Murdock

Page 82: Tria Giovan
Page 83: Roger Davies
Page 84: Pieter Estersohn
Page 85: Antoine Bootz
Page 86: Edmund Barr
Page 87: Hugh Stewart
Page 88: Jonn Coolidge
Page 89: Peter Murdock
Page 90: Laura Resen
Page 91: Eric Piasecki
Page 92: Pieter Estersohn
Page 93: Christopher Baker
Page 94: Simon Upton
Page 95: Eric Piasecki
Page 96: Vicente Wolf
Page 97: Pieter Estersohn
Page 98: Tria Giovan
Page 99: Jonn Coolidge
Page 100: Jonn Coolidge
Page 101: Antoine Bootz
Page 102: Peter Murdock
Page 103: Laura Moss
Page 104: Tim Street-Porter
Page 105: Tria Giovan
Page 106: Jonn Coolidge
Page 107: Eric Piasecki
Page 108: John Gould Bessler
Page 109: Pieter Estersohn
Page 110: Lisa Romerein
Page 111: Eric Piasecki
Page 112: Gordon Beall
Page 113: Karyn R. Millet
Page 114: Antoine Bootz
Page 115: Tria Giovan
Page 116: Ellen McDermott
Page 117: Eric Piasecki
Page 118: Roger Davies
Page 119: Karyn R. Millet

Page 120: Tria Giovan
Page 121: Grey Crawford
Page 122: Tim Street-Porter
Page 123: John Gould Bessler
Page 124: John M. Hall
Page 125: Eric Piasecki
Page 126: Tria Giovan
Page 127: Ken Hayden
Page 128: Pieter Estersohn
Page 129: Pieter Estersohn
Page 130: Nina Bramhall
Page 131 (both): John M. Hall
Pages 132–133: Lisa Romerein
Page 134: Eric Piasecki
Page 135: Jeff McNamara
Page 136: Darrin Haddad
Page 137: Eric Piasecki
Page 138: Tim Street-Porter
Page 139: Eric Piasecki
Page 140: Karyn R. Millet
Page 141: Chuck Baker
Page 142: Eric Piasecki
Page 143: Dominique Vorillon
Page 144: Grey Crawford
Page 145: Tria Giovan
Page 146: Ellen McDermott
Page 147: Frances Janisch
Page 148: Christopher Baker
Page 149: Christopher Baker
Page 150: Carlos Emilio
Page 151: Oberto Gili
Page 152: Don Freeman
Page 153: Ken Hayden
Page 154: John Gould Bessler
Page 155: Jack Thompson
Page 156 (left): Roger Davies
Page 156 (right): Don Freeman
Page 157: Pieter Estersohn

Page 319: Karyn R. Millet
Page 320: Tria Giovan
Page 321: Grey Crawford
Page 322: Tim Street-Porter
Page 323: Kerri McCaffety
Page 324: Eric Piasecki
Page 325: Frances Janisch
Page 326: Eric Piasecki
Page 327: Roger Davies
Page 328: J. Savage Gibson
Page 329: Eric Piasecki
Page 330: Jeff McNamara
Page 331: Tria Giovan
Page 332: Antoine Bootz
Page 333: Tim Street-Porter
Page 334: Eric Piasecki
Page 335: Frances Janisch
Page 336: Dominique Vorillon
Page 337: Laura Moss
Page 338: Ann Stratton
Page 339: John Gould Bessler
Page 340: Susan Gilmore
Page 341: Eric Piasecki
Page 342: Nina Bramhall
Page 343: John M. Hall
Pages 344–345: Victoria Pearson
Page 346: Michel Arnaud
Page 347: Simon Upton
Page 348: Paul Whicheloe
Page 349: Paul Whicheloe
Page 350: Simon Upton
Page 351: Ellen McDermott
Page 352: Tria Giovan
Page 353: Frances Janisch
Page 354: Eric Roth
Page 355: John Ellis
Page 356: J. Savage Gibson
Page 357: Oberto Gili
Page 358: John Gould Bessler
Page 359: Gordon Beall

Page 360: Karyn R. Millet
Page 361: Pieter Estersohn
Page 362: John Ellis
Page 363: Victoria Pearson
Page 364: Eric Piasecki
Page 365: Simon Upton
Page 366: Peter Murdock
Page 367: William Waldron
Page 368: John Gould Bessler
Page 369: Roger Davies
Page 370: Jeff McNamara
Page 371: Frances Janisch
Pages 372–373: Roger Davies
Page 374: John Gould Bessler
Page 375: Eric Piasecki
Page 376: J. Savage Gibson
Page 377: Andreas von Einsiedel
Page 378: Pieter Estersohn
Page 379: Ken Hayden
Page 380: Carlos Emilio
Page 381: Antoine Bootz
Page 382: Tria Giovan
Page 383: Frances Janisch
Page 384: Ray Kachatorian
Page 385: Eric Piasecki
Page 386: Pieter Estersohn
Page 387: Pieter Estersohn
Page 388: Christopher Baker
Page 389: Karyn R. Millet
Page 390: Don Freeman
Page 391: Frances Janisch
Page 392: John Gould Bessler
Page 393: Erik Kvalsvik
Page 394: Victoria Pearson
Page 395: Tria Giovan
Page 396: Tim Street-Porter
Page 397: Simon Upton
Page 398: Eric Piasecki
Page 399: Eric Piasecki
Page 400: Eric Piasecki

Page 401: Peter Murdock
Page 402: Peter Murdock
Page 403: John Gould Bessler
Page 404: Dominique Vorillon
Page 405: Charles Maraia
Page 406 (left): Dominique Vorillon
Page 406 (right): San An
Page 407: Eric Piasecki
Page 408: John Gould Bessler
Page 409: Christopher Baker
Page 410: Brendan Paul
Page 411: Grey Crawford
Page 412: Pieter Estersohn
Page 413: Tim Beddow
Page 414: Ken Hayden
Page 415: Nick Sargent
Page 416: John M. Hall
Page 417: Marion Brenner
Pages 418–419: Karyn R. Millet
Page 420: Grey Crawford
Page 421: Roger Davies
Page 422 (both): Eric Piasecki
Page 423: Edmund Barr
Page 424: Jeff McNamara
Page 425: Eric Piasecki
Page 426: Don Freeman
Page 427: Roger Davies
Page 428: Tria Giovan
Page 429: Tria Giovan
Page 430: Andreas von Einsiedel
Page 431: Dominique Vorillon
Page 432: Frances Janisch
Page 433: Paul Whicheloe
Page 434: Carlos Emilio
Page 435: Lisa Romerein
Page 436: John Ellis
Page 437: Gordon Beall
Page 438: Don Freeman
Page 439: Ken Hayden
Page 440: Roger Davies

Page 441: Brendan Paul
Page 442: Dominique Vorillon
Page 443: Charles Maraia
Page 444: Roger Davies
Page 445: J. Savage Gibson
Page 446: John Gould Bessler
Page 447: Brendan Paul
Page 448: Christopher Baker
Page 449: Dominique Vorillon
Page 450: Tria Giovan
Page 451: John M. Hall
Page 452 (left): Tria Giovan
Page 452 (right): Eric Piasecki
Page 453: Laura Resen
Page 454: Ken Hayden
Page 455: Charles Maraia
Page 456: Karyn R. Millet
Page 457: Jonathan Wallen
Page 458: Grey Crawford
Page 459: John Gould Bessler
Page 460: Gridley + Graves
Page 461: Tria Giovan
Page 462: Tria Giovan
Page 463: Eric Piasecki
Page 464: Karyn R. Millet
Page 465: Ray Kachatorian
Page 466: Jonathan Wallen
Page 467: Tim Street-Porter
Page 468: Karyn R. Millet
Page 469: Tim Street-Porter
Page 470: J. Savage Gibson
Page 471: Ray Kachatorian
Page 472: Kerri McCaffety
Page 473: Laura Moss

index